HELP FROM HEAVEN

Direct From Spirit: Living Beyond Your Beliefs

CONNIE FOX

Copyright © 2015 Connie Fox.

All rights reserved. No part of this book may be used or reproduced by any means, graphic, electronic, or mechanical, including photocopying, recording, taping or by any information storage retrieval system without the written permission of the publisher except in the case of brief quotations embodied in critical articles and reviews.

Balboa Press books may be ordered through booksellers or by contacting:

Balboa Press
A Division of Hay House
1663 Liberty Drive
Bloomington, IN 47403
www.balboapress.com
1 (877) 407-4847

Because of the dynamic nature of the Internet, any web addresses or links contained in this book may have changed since publication and may no longer be valid. The views expressed in this work are solely those of the author and do not necessarily reflect the views of the publisher, and the publisher hereby disclaims any responsibility for them.

The author of this book does not dispense medical advice or prescribe the use of any technique as a form of treatment for physical, emotional, or medical problems without the advice of a physician, either directly or indirectly. The intent of the author is only to offer information of a general nature to help you in your quest for emotional and spiritual well-being. In the event you use any of the information in this book for yourself, which is your constitutional right, the author and the publisher assume no responsibility for your actions.

Print information available on the last page.

ISBN: 978-1-4525-9927-4 (sc)
ISBN: 978-1-4525-9928-1 (e)

Balboa Press rev. date: 03/11/2015

Contents

Chapter 1	Jesus Defines a Pure Heart	1
Chapter 2	Jesus Defines Becoming Your True Self	3
Chapter 3	How to Develop More Trust in God	5
Chapter 4	Jesus Defines Religion	19
Chapter 5	Jesus Defines Love	23
Chapter 6	A Simple Way to Gain the Power of God	27
Chapter 7	Healing Principles Direct from Spirit	29
Chapter 8	Earth Devolving	37
Chapter 9	Mahatma Gandhi Speaks on Kindness	41
Chapter 10	Surrendering	43
Chapter 11	The Value of Prayer and a Deeper Knowledge of How to Pray	47
Chapter 12	Jesus Defines Self-Forgiveness	53
Chapter 13	Heal Emotional Pain with "Babaji's Work"	59
Chapter 14	The Heart Technique	65
Chapter 15	Why Jesus Gave Mette the Heart Technique	69
Chapter 16	Archangel Metatron Speaks on Pride	71
Chapter 17	Why People Tend to Resist Jesus	75
Chapter 18	Jesus Defines the Presence of God	77
Chapter 19	Jesus Defines the Process of Creation	79

Questions with Answers from Jesus 83
- The Issue of Being Gay and the Truth about Judging Other People 83
- The Reason Behind Child Molestation and How to Help .. 84
- Teaching Children about God 88
- How We Can Create an Enlightened Society 88
- The Benefits of Surrendering Control 89
- Soul Desires Versus Ego Desires 90
- Surrender – It's All You Really Need 93
- Words to Describe God 94
- Without Beliefs, Who Are You? 95

- Jesus Interprets from the Bible 97
- Was Your Death Really Our Salvation? 101
- Jesus Defines Sin 101
- Recommended Reading From Jesus 101
- I Want a Daily Spiritual Practice – So Why Don't I Do it? 101
- Why Jesus Was Born into the Jewish Faith 102
- Why the Holocaust Happened 103
- Destiny and Free Will 104
- The Belief that Spirit Communication is Evil 105
- Believing in Satan 107
- The Nature of an Animal's Soul 108
- After We Die, Do We Remain in Heaven For Eternity? ... 108
- Is There Only One True Path to God? 108

Extended Summary of Babaji's Work 111
Brief Summary of Babaji's Work 115
What Mette has to say about the "Heart Technique" 117
In Closing from the Author 121
Experience The Peace, Love and Bliss I Am 123
Why You Are Not Happy 127
The Life Piece [as shown on book cover] 131

ACKNOWLEDGEMENTS

To my mother Susan Fox, you are and always have been my greatest blessing. Thank you mom for all of your editing services! I give many thanks to my friend David Hoffman for enticing me to begin this project. It was Mette Bergmann and Bent Breitenstein who made the entire endeavor possible – my undying gratitude to you both. To my dear friend Sonja Bednar for creating the cover of this book. To Charlie DeMichele, Cynthia Fisher, Bill Shae, Jonathon Besdine, Dan Werner, Ron Boiuso, Joshua Louis, Mark Gilbert, Joan Cehak, Pam Stewart and each and every one of my special friends at the Oasis. I am eternally grateful to you all. Without your unconditional love and support and caring enough to share, I would not have been able to complete this book. In sharing this book with everyone, I also share a part of you.

Foreword

While writing my first book, *"The Power of You"*, I was struggling to accept the unacceptable. It was now unlikely I would ever have the children I so long desired. Meeting my basic financial needs became a real challenge for the first time in my life. Slowly I began to realize I had lived my entire life for a future that would not manifest as planned.

Due to a decade of severe health problems I was stuck in deep anger and resentment of all I had lost; of all that could have been. There was no way I could accept my new unwanted circumstances. My youth and abundant financial security were now lost to a pattern of continuous fear and panic which had developed in my perception. To begin with, I felt very much a victim from the effects of being mercury poisoned. After a long, arduous and expensive recovery, I was confronted by a life in poverty and no hope for the husband and family I had intended. I remained in a state of deep self-pity and anger toward God.

At the end of transcribing *"Babaji's Conversations"* from my first book, my life got worse. I became homeless and suicidal. From what I will call the grace of God, I learned the value of surrender. Only because life's events granted me the gift of desperation, did I follow through and surrender as described in these pages. That was nearly a year ago and I would now like to share with you where I am today.

I live with a solid foundation of true peace. I define true peace as the result of developing intentional contact with God. You may think it odd that I, who could directly communicate with most any spirit, as well as with God, had not already gained a deep and personal spiritual relationship by means of my communication gift. It is rather extraordinary in itself, being able to fluidly converse with consciousness at will. Logically, I knew I was never alone; God was always there for me. Yet, I first needed to create the *willingness* to let go of my punishing, limited beliefs.

This was a whole new way of thinking for me. I had always prided myself as being a self-reliant and independent "go-getter". I never knew I was so attached to controlling my life until I tried to let go of that control. You see, I was always so competent at achieving my goals, that is, until I wasn't anymore. And the reality of such helplessness brought me to my knees.

I gained an unfamiliar inner peace, gratitude and joy that result only from relying on a source higher than one's self. No longer do I think that happiness occurs in my life due to outer circumstances going the right way. This was an incredibly challenging transformation to accept. It required surrendering all that I believed about myself and life as I knew it.

It is my humble opinion that you may avoid much of the pain and loss in your own life by applying the simple truths found in this book. They were all given to me freely, none were consciously chosen by me. I remain grateful for the loving intelligence who spoke through me. I am confident that you would not be reading this now if you were not ready to discover and deepen your own inner peace which comes only from relying on a source of power higher than yourself.

I have adopted a new way of living thanks to the many gifts of pain and loss. My life is now one of following my soul's direction rather than leading against it. That has made all the difference.

Connie Fox
February 14, 2014
North Palm Beach, Florida

Jesus Defines a Pure Heart

The Bible often talks about having a pure heart. It emphasizes the importance of having a pure heart, yet its meaning has been misinterpreted. So, I would like to define what a pure heart is and why it is important to have one.

A pure heart has nothing to do with sex. It has nothing to do with religion. It has nothing to do with one's beliefs. A pure heart is a heart that has nothing but pure love; being fully loving to one's self and to others. A pure heart has no more pain and no more fear. A pure heart is a healed heart. This is all there is to defining a pure heart.

Judgment is the only thing that causes a heart to become "un-pure"; that is, filled with pain and fear. You need to learn how to accept the existence of your fear. When you do not accept fear, know that this is the ego playing a clever trick on you in order to resist the reality of the fear. It is avoidance. This is to keep you in ignorance of the fear. The ego does not want you to be aware of the fear, lest you face it and thereby eliminate it.

The only way the ego can resist fear is by attaching it to something - something outside of you. So you become focused on, that is identified with, the outer judgment rather than the inner fear. This is how you remain ignorant. This is how you stagnate, stuck in your judgments. This hidden technique of the ego hides the awareness of your true-self - God.

Fear causes attachment and attachment causes fear, and then more fear. Judgment rushes in to rescue you from facing your fear. You place your fear outside of yourself onto someone or something else. In this way, you avoid facing the fear, feeling the fear and dealing with the fear.

Judgment is the tool used to mask and resist the fear; it is ego-identification. Love is reduced from the very first fear that you resist. Your ego is born upon your first judgment (resistance to fear). You begin to create a pattern of responses that you become familiar with in the form of judgment. Resistance to fear is now firmly established and judgments continue automatically. Once a judgment is created it continues to reinforce itself, weeding out love as it goes.

More and more fear replaces love. In this way you further deepen a resistance to love – u*nknowingly.* This is how you no longer experience a pure heart, which is your true heritage. How do you turn around a pattern of such resistance that has become so familiar that you know of no other way? You become consciously aware of when you are judging.

The most important part to becoming aware of your resistance to loving is to not resist fear. This means not to judge it. Your judgment is so deep-rooted that you need to intentionally, consciously watch yourself. When I say watch yourself, I mean literally watch yourself. As a third party, observe yourself during any activity. Increase your awareness of your judgments by p*aying attention to your judgments.* This is the beginning of creating a new pattern of thinking, perception, feeling and action. It is a new pattern toward re-developing a pure heart.

Jesus Defines Becoming Your True Self

I want you to clearly understand the definition of your "true-self".

It is your true-self that existed with a pure heart before you developed your fears. And it is your true-self you will return to when your fears are fully healed.

It is much easier to transition to your true-self's awareness if you have a definitive understanding of what your true-self means. It is easier to accomplish if you have the willingness to want it. And you cannot want it, if you do not know what it is.

You are going to become your true-self again. But, the when is all up to you. If you knew how much you were missing in your direct experience of life, you would have no other priority but to become it – your true self - God-realized.

Most of you walk through life like sleep-walking zombies, cut off from "life". You are alive, but you do not live fully. "Life" is the very essence of who you are. Yet, you have not known it for so long that you have forgotten what you are missing.

Living the "Zombie" life means feeling alone or empty of God's presence, not understanding there is more – much more. You have accustomed yourself to the life-less life, having become numb. Even what you may consider to be happiness and contentment is nothing in comparison to what you can experience. I am referring to fullness of life.

An incomplete life is one that is missing the awareness of God. To grow out of an incomplete life, your acknowledgement is needed.

> *If you do not understand what God is*
> *Through your direct experience,*
> *You are not experiencing fullness of life.*

Using the intellect – the mind – to define your version of who God is or is not according to your beliefs, will not get you there. It is more challenging to attain the experience of living at a level of 'more' if you do not even know that 'more' exists. Know that I want you to enjoy fullness of life.

When you notice a feeling of something missing, recognize it for what it is. It is not a new job you are missing, it is not a new partner, it is not a new car, it is not a bigger, better, higher person, place or thing. It is God that is missing in your awareness.

If you knew how much pain you continue to create for yourselves, year after year, lifetime after lifetime, you would not be able to withstand the regret. This is the truth of why you have been avoiding God. Know that if you became realized of all that you have missed, you would then be filled with the love, peace and joy needed to instantly dissolve all regrets from the past.

I want you to experience fullness of life. Please do *"Babaji's Work"* and *"The Heart Technique"* [later in this book]. It is simple. It takes a very small amount of time each day and you will grow toward the experience of being your true-self again. Mahavatar Babaji* and I are giving you a way to experience fullness of life. Please take advantage of it.

---

* Spiritual teacher, Mahavatar Babaji, a devotee of Christ.

How to Develop More Trust in God

From Archangel Gabriel:
Trust is hard for the mind to understand. The mind can only identify through the five physical senses. Trust comes from beyond the five physical senses. The only way trust can be genuinely developed is through surrendering your fears. Trust accompanies a fearless heart. A fearless heart accompanies a fearless mind. So, start with the mind. Change your thinking. How do you change your fear-based thinking? You do it by intentionally thinking thoughts that are less fearful. You have to re-train your mind's way of thinking.

> *You are controlled like a puppet from your thoughts.*
> *That is, until you are fearless.*
> *Be able to think differently.*

This is the only way to salvation (freedom from fear). Jesus cannot be your server without your willingness to change your thoughts. If you continue to want to think the same, you will continue to feel fear – and more fear and more fear, again and again. Eventually, you will give up the fight and surrender your fear – bit by bit by bit.

Why would you want to reach fearlessness by such a slow, arduous route? You don't. So, why pretend like you do? Just let it go. It is as simple as that. Choose to feel differently about something you fear. How do you change feeling fearful to not feeling fearful? You think differently about it. There is no way around this.

I will give you ten examples so you can understand how to develop more trust. Again, trust accompanies having less fear. You cannot trust more without decreasing your fear and you cannot feel less fear about something unless you think less fearfully about it:

1. a) "I'm afraid I will become homeless. I am barely getting by as it is. Something is going to happen that's going to sink me in. How can it not? Extra needs come up. A doctor's appointment, a car repair. There are so many needs I have. What am I going to do? There is nothing I can do. I'm doing all I can already. My life is already a struggle. It's barely worth living as it is. There's no escaping my life. I should have made better decisions. I screwed up. But it's too late now. I cannot go back in time. I blew it. I settled for less. But, I did the best I could. I did not know any better. I wasn't given everything I needed to know to make better choices. That's not my fault. But, I'm the one that's stuck with the consequences. I'm never going to have a great life. I'm just going to have to keep living like this. I hate my life. If I had a better life, I could be happy. I deserve more and I will never get it. Why won't God help me."

Instead, intentionally think this a dozen or more times a day. I do not say you must believe it. Just think it.

1. b) "God, I have a problem. I am really struggling financially. I am not able to make more money right now. I'm doing the best I can already and I do not know what to do. I need more of my needs met. A lot more of my needs met. Please help me God. Please help me know what to do or what not to do. I'm afraid. Please take this worry of mine from me. I give it to You now. Please take my present situation from me and improve it greatly. I trust in You God. I know You hear me now. I am going to trust You. I know You can do for me what I cannot do for myself. Thank you for bringing me a solution to this situation. Please help me trust in You more and more each day. I am willing to change something if needed. Please show me the way. Thank you."

2. a) "I'm sick. I have a terminal disease. I am very sick. What on earth am I going to do? My doctors have told me I'm going to die and maybe suffer a long time. Why is this happening to me? How can this be happening to me? I don't deserve this. I'm a good person. There's nothing anyone can do for me except help me cope. I do not want to

cope through life. I want to be happy and feel good. This cannot be happening to me. I had different plans. This is not right. I'm supposed to be happy. Many other people are happy. Don't I deserve to be happy? I'm not a bad person. I'm going to lose myself. Will my friends still want me around? Will my partner? I don't have a partner. I'm going to have to go through this alone. I'm so afraid. I don't deserve this. I need help. But, I can't get any. I'm stuck with this. I want to die right here and now. I don't want to suffer. I shouldn't have to suffer. How could God let this happen to me? What's wrong with me that I don't deserve a happy, healthy life? What am I going to do? How can I get through this? I can't handle this."

Instead, intentionally think this a dozen or more times a day:

2. b) "God, I am sick; very sick. I have a terminal disease. I do not think any doctor can really help me. My doctors said I'm going to get worse until I die. But, I can't die. I know I can't die. The real me is eternal. My body is just a host for my spirit to experience for a while. There are still so many things I want to do. I don't want to leave my family. They will miss me greatly. I do not want them to go through my loss. That's the last thing I want for them. God, I do not know how to handle this. I need Your help. I cannot go through this without You. Please help me trust in You more. I need to feel Your strength and comfort. I am afraid. Please change my health for the better if that is Your will. If it is not, I trust in You. I know there are no mistakes. I may not understand why this is happening, but I know You do. I accept dying earlier than expected. I know You will be there the moment I pass, because I am asking You to. And I know You will always be there for someone who asks for You. Please give me the strength I need to handle this situation as You would like me to. Please help me make this easier for my loved ones. I know this time will pass and who I really am can never die. Thank you for helping me through this time God. Deep down I know I have nothing to fear. Physical death is a natural part of life. I know You will take good care

of my family. Help us all get through this time with more trust and faith in You. Thank you God."

3. a) "Oh no. My purse was stolen out of my car. What am I going to do? I just cashed my paycheck. It's two week's worth of pay. Oh no. This cannot be. It has all my credit cards and my driver's license. It had my social security card and personal information. What if they steal my identity? This is horrible. I need a drink. This world sucks. There are such lousy people in this world. I've never stolen anything. This is not fair to have this happen to me. Why did this happen to me? I don't deserve this. My whole day is ruined. My whole week is ruined. My whole month is ruined. How am I going to pay my rent now? I'm not. Oh my gosh, what am I going to do? This sucks. My life sucks. Maybe I can get the police to help me. But, they're not going to do anything. I hope that person suffers for what s/he did to me. S/he deserves to. My money is very important to me. I work so hard for my money. I shouldn't have to deal with this. Life is so unfair."

Instead, intentionally think this a dozen or more times a day:

3. b) "God, my purse was just stolen out of my car. And it had two week's worth of my pay. I needed that money to pay my rent. I'm going to be very inconvenienced needing to get another driver's license, social security card and credit cards. I don't know what to do to pay my rent now. Will You please bring me the help I need to get my rent paid? I do not have any idea how to do it. But, I know You will bring me what I need. And if I don't get my rent paid on time, I know You will give me the support I need to get through this ok. I trust in You God. I know there's a good reason for everything, whether or not I know what it is. Help me surrender any anger or hate I have toward the person that just stole my purse. Please take it from me. I cannot help feeling this anger right now. But, that's ok, I am human and I have human feelings. I am grateful for all that I have. I have a home, a car, a job, I have people in my life that I care about. I really am blessed God and I thank you for helping me let

this go. I pray that the person that stole my purse finds a better way of living their life. Please help him/her God. S/he must need Your help. I'm going to go home and love my family. Thank you God for me and my car being ok."

4. a) "A man just became belligerent with me. He is absolutely crazy. I should have called the police. Why didn't I call the police? I'm so dumb. What a SOB he was. If I had a boyfriend, I'd have him go kick his butt. He needs a significant beating. He should be fired from his job. He's a sick man screaming and hollering like that. And I was a normal, calm person. Why do I get stuck with people like this? It's just not right that I, of all people had to deal with this guy. What is wrong with me that this stuff happens to me? God doesn't care about me. He lets me be mistreated from one person to the next. It's just not right. I'm kind and polite to people. My co-worker is always so rude and people just cater to her. I'm nice and I just get treated like a doormat. Why do I deserve this? There must be something wrong with me to attract people like this."

Instead, intentionally think this a dozen or more times a day:

4. b) "God, that man just screamed at me. He was absolutely crazy. Why did this happen to me God? I know nothing is an accident. There must be something valuable for me to learn here. I will be open to learning what it is. Please help me understand why I needed this experience. He made me very upset God. Will You please take my upset feelings from me? I don't want to hang onto them because they're starting to make me feel bad about myself. But, I know it is nothing to take personally. That person just has some serious anger issues. God, please help heal his pain and anger. I wish him well. And I know I will be given the knowledge I need as to why this happened to me. I am open to being more compassionate too, if that is what I need. God, thank you for helping me receive what I need to help me learn how to love myself and others as You do. Help me feel closer to You every day. Thank you God."

5. "My wife cheated on me. Oh my Gosh. No, no, no. This cannot be. This is impossible. I trusted her and she betrayed me in the very worst way. I knew I shouldn't have married her. I had a feeling she was a lying cheater. But, I cannot believe it. How could she do this to me? I loved her. I trusted her. I gave her years of my life. I want her to pay for this. She should know what it's like to feel this way. I'm going to make her pay for this. She deserves to pay for what she's done. I'm going to take everything she's got. She got everything from me anyway. I've supported her. I've helped her get to where she is now. And this is how I get paid? I don't deserve this. I'm so stupid. How could I have married her? All the sacrifices I made for nothing. My life will never be the same. She destroyed my life."

Instead, intentionally think this a dozen or more times a day:

5. b) "Oh my Gosh, my wife cheated on me. I cannot believe this. How could she have done this to me? I love her. I have been good to her. I trusted her. I don't know what I'm going to do. I feel like a victim. I don't know why this is happening to me. My whole life has been different than I thought it was. My future is going to be different than I planned. I don't know how to handle this. God, please help me. I need Your help. Please help me know what to do. I don't know what to do right now, but I know You will show me the way. My pain is so deep, I can barely handle it. Please help me heal my pain. Please help me see what I need to see that created this experience for me. It is not my fault, I know. But, I know there is something that I am missing in my awareness that caused me to attract this experience. I am willing to see my part in this. I know there are no victims in this world. I know this is happening for a reason. It is not because I am being punished, I know it is because I need to learn something that is blocking my awareness to fully loving myself. I am very hurt God. Please help comfort me with Your peace. Please help my wife become more whole-minded. I know she is learning something needed from this experience also. My life is going to be different

now and I need Your help to get through this time. I know this is a blessing in disguise. I need to learn how to love myself more. I know that's the underlying reason for going through hurtful experiences. I thank you for this opportunity to grow closer to You. All I need is You. This pain and emptiness is really because I do not feel more of Your love and fullness. Perhaps this is a time for me to grow closer to You. I know what my wife did is really because of something she is missing inside, which is You. And I know we are all doing the best we can at the level of awareness we are at. But, I am so hurt and angry at her. Please help me forgive my wife. Please help me forgive myself. I am willing to God. Thank you."

6. a) "I got fired today. I'm going to lose everything. This cannot be happening to me. I had a feeling this was going to happen. I never get what I deserve. I am better at what I do than everyone in there. But, my boss does not care. He just doesn't like me because I don't kiss his butt like the others do. I have self-respect and so I get fired for it. This is outrageous. I hate that guy. He's a lousy boss. He lets his ego get in the way of making good decisions. He doesn't deserve to be a boss. How does someone like him get to be a boss? Life is so unfair. I think I may complain to his boss and let him know how he really is. His boss doesn't even know how inept he is. He should know. I gave my heart and soul to this job. I worked harder than anyone here. This is so not right that this is happening to me. I deserve so much better. What am I going to do? What if I don't get another job soon? I could lose my house. I have kids to feed. What if I fail at being a good husband and father? I cannot handle this. My wife is going to be so upset. I'm not good enough for my wife. She deserves to have security in her life. Maybe I'm a loser after all. I thought these days were behind me and here I am again, needing to start all over and at my age? Oh my gosh, this is a nightmare."

Instead, intentionally think this a dozen or more times a day:

6. b) "I got fired from a job I was happy at. I am so disappointed. I thought I was going to be there a long time. Plans change and I know this happening is going to bring something even better than I planned. I am still really disappointed though. But, sometimes God has something planned for me that I do not know about. I accept this change. I know God will take care of everything. I trust God. I know there's a good reason for this. God, please help me trust in You more. I'm feeling afraid, so I know I need to trust You more. I know You can turn this into a blessing in disguise. I give this situation to You God. Please help me know what to do from here because right now, I have no idea. I will pay attention to the guidance that comes my way. I trust that all will be well. I have nothing to fear with You in my life. I know You will take care of everything that is beyond my control. I thank you for this opportunity to improve my life. I know something good is going to come from this. This may seem like a travesty now, but I know You have something better planned for me and I accept Your blessings. Please help my wife feel safe and secure and have trust in You God. We will get through this time of change with Your help. Everything will be okay and I am grateful for everything I have. Thank you God."

7. a) I want this opportunity so badly. If I don't get this, I am going to be so mad. I will be devastated. I've worked my whole life for this opportunity and I deserve it. I know a lot of people who got to where they are and they really don't deserve it – not as much as I do, anyway. I've had to fight and struggle my way through life. Life has not been easy for me. If I get this opportunity, I'll be able to be happy. I've waited a long time to get where I am now and I am not going to accept less. I shouldn't have to. I should be able to have a good life like many other people do. I've been given one challenge after another and I'm not going to take it any more. If I don't get this opportunity, I don't know what I'm going to do. I don't want to struggle my way

through life anymore. I just want to be happy. I want to have a good life. I deserve this. Gosh, I hope I get this. What if I don't?"

Instead, intentionally think this a dozen or more times a day:

7 b) "God, thank you for bringing this opportunity my way. I hope I get it. I feel it would enhance my life so much and I ask You to make it Your will that I get this opportunity. But, if it is not Your will and I don't get it, I trust and know that You will bring me another opportunity just as good or better. I get my peace, security and love from You, not from the circumstances in my life. I know that if I am dependent on my life's circumstances to be happy, I will never be happy for long. Life in this physical world is very fleeting. Circumstances will always continue to change. But, if I am able to accept whatever circumstances come my way and rely on You for my peace and happiness, I need not feel overwhelmed by such challenges. I will not perceive them as challenging anymore because I trust in You to bring me everything I need, as I need it. You are the only thing that is not fleeting. Only You can bring me true and everlasting peace and happiness. Although, I am not completely fearless yet, I trust in You God. I know that my fear prevents me from having more trust in You. So, I give You my fear and ask You to replace it with more trust. I am willing to let go of more of my fear. I know that the more I trust in You, the more fearless I become. I recognize that I am attached to getting this opportunity. Thank you God for all I have, for all you have given me."

8. a) "I cannot believe I still have not met my soul mate. I'm not asking for that much, am I? Millions of people have a loving partner to share their life with to have children with. Why not me? What's wrong with me? There's nothing wrong with me. I'm so disappointed with my life. Nothing comes easy for me. Why do so many people get to experience that and I don't? I see so many bad parents that have children. It's just not right. I would be a wonderful parent. I don't understand why God keeps me from finding a good partner. My

friend is a horrible husband and he's got the most loving, beautiful wife. That sucks and I'm not going to take it anymore. I'm going to be a jerk to women from now on. Then, I'll get a good woman in my life. It's the bad guys that seem to always get a good woman and they don't even appreciate it. Women seem to like jerks. But, I'm not a jerk. Life is so unfair. Am I going to have to live alone for the rest of my life? Unwanted and alone? That would be horrible. I cannot accept that. That is not how it's supposed to be. Maybe I should just accept less, rather than waiting for someone I really want to marry. Why is my biggest nightmare happening to me? This shouldn't be happening."

Instead, intentionally think this a dozen or more times a day:

8. b) "I still have not found my soul mate. I thought I would have been married by now or even have children by now. I wish I had someone special to share my life with and to have a family with. I am ready for that. Since that has not yet happened, I need to put my attention on enjoying what I do have. I have great friends and my dog is awesome. God must want me to enjoy this more fully right now. I'm sure I am going to have a wife and family if it is God's will. If not, I will be very disappointed, but I will have to accept that and I will. I know that God may have a purpose for me that is different than what I think is best for me. And I trust God's judgment more than my own. God knows what I do not. God, please help me surrender my fear of not having a wife or family. I ask You to bring me a compatible wife and family if it is Your will. But, if it is not, please help me accept that with ease and grace and guide me to what will fulfill me more in my life. I am open to Your will God. I trust you fully. I know it's not happening for a reason and I do not have to know what that reason is right now – because I do trust in You. If there is something I am doing to prevent myself from attracting an ideal partner, please show me what that is. I am willing to change something if needed. Thank you for all the love I do have in my life from my family, friends and my dog. I am grateful to have them in my life."

9. a) "I am in so much physical pain and suffering. This injury/illness has been making my life miserable for so long now. I hate my life. I want to die. I cannot live like this anymore. My life is not worth living like this. I have no life. God has abandoned me. God has totally betrayed me. How could God leave me like this? How can He really care about me to let me suffer like this? Is God punishing me for something? There is no God or He just doesn't care about me at all. I don't know why this is happening to me. I don't deserve this. No one should have to live like this. I wouldn't wish this on my worst enemy. Kill me, God. Have some mercy and at least let me die. End my pain and suffering. If You don't, I will. I cannot continue living like this. I do not and will not accept this anymore."

Instead, intentionally think this a dozen or more times a day.

9. b) "God, I am in so much pain, I do not think I have the strength to go on like this anymore. My life is precious to me and my loved ones and I would like to experience and do more good in this world. I want to be more useful to You God. I know that is my ultimate purpose - to serve You through helping others. I know this experience I am going through is somehow going to help me learn how I can do that more and in a way that I enjoy that gives me more fulfillment in life and deepens my love for myself and others. I do not know how, but I know this time of challenge will eventually end and I ask You to help me get through this time. I need Your help to continue God. I am losing all hope. I ask You to give me more hope and courage. I need You, God, now more than ever. If it is Your will, please help me heal what I need to heal. I will be open to new knowledge that may be helpful. Help me be more aware of what I need. I trust You are and will continue giving me what I need throughout each day. If it is not Your will to heal this right now, please give me more strength to endure this time. I know this experience is helping me learn something that will be invaluable to me. I know You coordinate every minute detail of what transpires in Your world and in my life. Often times, I do not understand the good that is going to come from painful experiences. And I know You

cannot and do not make mistakes. I am having trouble accepting this, but I am willing to. I fully surrender this injury/illness to You now. It is in Your hands now God, not mine, for I recognize I have no control to fix this right now. The sooner I accept Your will, what presently is, the sooner this experience will not be needed. Please help me cope with more trust and faith in You and with more ease and grace. Please give me more of Your strength and peace. Choosing to be angry and fearful prevents me from allowing Your peace and love to enliven within me, as well as Your guidance and direction. So, please take my anger and fear. I give it to You now. Thank you for the support I do have right now. I am grateful for it. Please show me the way."

10. a) "I'm an addict. I'm addicted to drugs/alcohol (food, gambling, sex, working, texting, stealing, worrying, abusive relationships, drama, etc). I can't stop. I know it's causing problems in my life but I just can't stop. It's not my fault I'm addicted to this kind of thinking and behavior. It's my parent's fault. It's God's fault too. Anyone that had my life would have developed this addiction too. I've had a lousy life. God gave me a life that sucks. No wonder I developed this addiction. I think I hate God for giving me the life I've had. He can go to hell for all I care. So can my mom/dad/spouse. Screw them. God supposedly loves all His children, but He certainly doesn't give a damn about me. I'm a good person, but I am human. So, I'm not perfect. A lot of people in the world had a good life. Why not me? It's so not fair. I'm worthless now. I can keep _____ if I want to. It's nobody's business but my own. But, I know I'm screwed up and there's nothing I can do about it. I want to be a better person, but I literally just can't stop this. I am doomed. My life is ruined now. There is no hope for me. I will never be free. It's too late for me."

Instead, intentionally think this a dozen or more times a day:

10. b) "God, I'm an addict. I'm addicted to _____. I recognize this fully and I don't know what to do. I simply cannot stop for some reason. It is not within my power to give up this self-damaging

addiction. It's hurting me and my life and other people that I care about. I need Your help God. Only You have the power to relieve me of this obsession I have with this addiction. I am sorry for all of the people I have hurt God. I am sorry for the wrongs I have done to myself and others. I am afraid. I realize I cannot free myself of this problem without Your divine intervention. I am willing to change, I just don't know how. I am willing to grow. I am ready to live my life with You, rather than alone. So I am asking You to help me God. I need Your help. I know I am damaged goods now and I cannot fix myself without You. I know that only You have the power to heal me. I am willing to change God. Please show me what I need to know or do to be free of this. Being off track in life brings pain, and I am in deep pain and utterly broken. I have not learned how to live my life with You as the active director. But with Your help, I am willing to change my ways. I am willing. I will wait and do my best to pay attention to Your lead now. I feel so much guilt and shame God. I think I hate myself. I hate who I have become. I feel worthless. Please help me love and forgive myself God. Please help me love and forgive others more, including You. I am sorry God, but I have so much anger and resentment. I feel rejected and abandoned by You. I feel that You don't care about me to let me suffer like this. I need You God. I want to know You. Please help me get to know You. I just need to know how. Please give me the strength I need and show me the way to freedom from this horrible _____. Thank you for this gift of desperation. I know that this is what it took to get me to this point of willingness to let it go and surrender it to You, my higher power. Thank you for the many support groups and all those people who are there to help me. Thank you God".

Pay attention to your inner dialogue. *Write your inner dialogue down.* Re-write it with an open, trusting and loving heart. Say it to yourself at least a dozen times a day. Do not negate it by verbally contradicting it to others. Always ask God to help you with what you need. Thank Him in advance for bringing you what you need. Tell Him you are open to receiving His guidance. Tell Him you want to trust in Him more. Tell Him what you are grateful for.

This will re-train your thinking. This will open your heart to being more loving to yourself and others. This will strengthen you and bring you peace and surrender to what you are resisting much more easily. This will help you learn how to develop more trust in God.

Create a less fearful, more trusting life by changing how you think. It all starts there. When you intentionally try to trust in God explicitly, by being willing to change your thinking, the power, love, peace and grace of God will enter your perception and heart. What you think and feel creates your life. Know this and take responsibility for what you create.

JESUS DEFINES RELIGION
Connie Asks; Jesus Answers

We have books like the Bible, the Torah, the Bhagavad Gita, the Tao, and other holy books. Would you say these Holy Scriptures are from God or from man?
Books and all sources of teaching come from man's level of awareness; from their belief system, their level of understanding. Some are highly aware, some not so highly aware. Some are more in alignment with truth, some less. I would like to give you my definition of religion.

My definition of religion is an organization that deciphers a source of knowledge according to their level of awareness. This includes what their already formed belief systems are. The purpose of religions is genuine. People get together with a purpose of trying to help others be with God, either while living or after the death of their bodies. Their intention is a good one. Yet many religions get caught up in what to believe about God rather than how to experience God.

Beliefs are never going to get one to "Heaven". It is the heart that brings one to salvation, understanding there is no separation after all, no separation from God in the first place, and no true separation from others.

Seeking God, peace, love, joy or wholeness means you feel separate from these qualities. Feeling separate from these means your belief systems prevent you from realizing them. You are never separate from them. Belief systems are not who you are. Experiencing more love is what your goal needs to be.

> *Trying to convert others into certain beliefs*
> *will actually hold you back from the*
> *experience of more love.*

It creates more separation; the distancing of yourself from love. Unity thinking leads to the feeling (experience) of more love.

So, I would like to invite you to form a 'new religion'; one that is not a religion but is a supportive group that helps to promote people to experience more love. This is My goal for religion. Beliefs about who or what God is, or what I represent, is merely a belief.

**A Belief about God is not what you need.
Experiencing more love is what you need.**

So, I will discuss certain ways for you to learn how to love more. Love is an energy that is the same as your spirit energy. This is "life". This is the Source of all creation. It is our Father and it is in every atom of the universe. Creation energy, life energy, My love which is in each of you, is pure love energy. Love energy flows through the heart, not the mind. Any belief will greatly limit the experience of more love. Anything from the mind is limited. A mind does not love, the heart does.

How do you expand your heart? By being more like Me – all loving, all compassionate and all non-judgmental. Giving what you have brings more of it back to you. You may give something helpful or not helpful; love-based or fear-based. Your only intention should be love-based. This means to give love.

Extend love to others as much as you can, not your beliefs.

Love is so natural when you let go of the ego's judgment. Judgment is not love-based. It is fear-based and separation-based. Love others, help others and be accepting of others whatever their beliefs are. Their beliefs are not who they are. Please understand this. Beliefs are not who you are either. You want to experience more of who you are (love), not believe something more.

You have an opportunity to love more with every living being you come across. Do not waste these precious opportunities to experience more love by trying to define, form or change another's belief system. Just give them love. Think of how you can be kind to them, help them, promote their happiness and joy, and experience their love with your love. Every time you extend love to others you deepen your connection to My love, to our Father's love, to the love that you are. This is how you experience more and more love until you reach Heaven.

Heaven is a state of awareness. Being fully aware of the love that you are is being in the "Kingdom of Heaven". Some of you also call this enlightenment or God consciousness. You can experience Heaven while in the physical body now, not only when in the afterlife (non-physical realm). Simply just love. Love is being kind, caring and compassionate. Put your love into action. A religion with this as the focus, rather than their beliefs being the focus, is my definition of a helpful religion.

JESUS DEFINES LOVE

A lot of talk about love has been taking place a very long time. I would like to define love from my awareness. Love is a form of energy. Your science teaches that every atom in the universe is living, moving and always changing energy. I agree. All forms of energy in your physical universe are as such. Yet, there are different forms of energy.

Love is a different form of energy. It is always the same. It is pure stillness, pure peace, pure bliss and pure love. This love energy is the Source of all creation. Its' creations are changeable, but not the Source of creation.

Anything in your physical world consists of the form of energy that is always moving, always changing. It never stays the same. It is not 'true' reality in the sense that it does not last. It is a temporary manifestation of the quality of your love energy. All of you create physical reality on earth from your own energy. This is what I want to discuss with you.

The *amount* of love energy flowing through your heart creates your physical world. The manifestation of your inner energy becomes your physical environment; the living, moving, changing energy that makes up your universe; every atom in your universe.

If you do not learn how to love more, the quality of your environment on earth will continue to deteriorate, as it has been doing for a long time. This is why I am defining love for you. I want to help you understand that love is essential for you to continue living on earth. The level of love flowing through a majority of people's hearts on this planet is so little, that you are about to unknowingly cause self-destruction.

Your spirit never dies, but your bodies will if you do not start learning how to bring more love-flow through your hearts, through your being. Those who do not quickly begin to love more will need to be reborn into another physical existence.

Earth is ready to evolve now. If you are not ready to evolve with it you cannot remain here. The other physical existence that some will be going to, allows them to continue evolving. It is not like earth. It is like what you might describe as a 'dungeon-type' planet.

I am speaking to you through Connie to give you another opportunity to choose love rather than fear. This time, it will be your body's death, not mine, should you choose fear. Not even I can make this decision for you, for you have your own free will.

A time is coming soon that will bring forms of destruction to this planet. This will remove the people who choose fear. I would like to introduce specific suggestions for how to be able to protect your selves from the coming destruction and rebuild an enlightened society around the globe; how to bring love, peace, harmony, independent living and enlightenment on earth.

Suggestion #1: Communities need to be developed from people who want to love more; who want to evolve spiritually; to become enlightened and help others do the same.

Suggestion #2: These communities need to become self-sufficient, needing no one outside the community to survive. This includes everything.

Suggestion #3: The ideal size of the communities would house 200 people, not much more than 300.

1st Topic: Building
Let's now start with topics of discussion. The first topic is about the building of a community. You need at least 100 acres of property, the more northern in your country (America) the better. It needs to be

a few miles or more away from any town or city. There should be a town center created in the center of this new community.

There should be teaching rooms for children and adults. Adults will be learning whatever you wish but should include sharing experiences to support and promote spiritual understanding and growth. There should be a room or two for each department. The departments needed are as follows:

- Farming/gardening
- A veterinarian's office, dental office and doctor's office with two individuals of each.
- A grounds keeper office (property manager)
- Protection and security

Other rooms/offices should include laborers, technicians, builders; what they need to build and repair things. This is all that is needed. But, add rooms of interest you may want. Housing structures should be gathered around your preferred design from around the town center extending outward.

2nd Topic: Food
Food needs to be fully provided from within the community. Have a few or more people that understand organic gardening, including greenhouse gardening and the raising of animals if desired (for food). Prepare, plant and harvest what you need for food.

3rd Topic: Air
Air quality will become denser at particular times that will last for days or weeks. This is from warfare contamination. If in the right location there will not be live bacteria or viruses, but not ideally clean air. Every home should have a basement with effective air filters to stay in during these select periods of time. There is no other concern about this topic.

4th Topic: Water
The property needs an underground water source and a water filtration system that is reliable.

5th Topic: Power
You need to provide your own power source that is not dependent on anything outside the community. Have a few experts that are knowledgeable about alternative power sources be a part of the community. Every home should have a wood burning stove that may also be used to heat the home if needed.

There is nothing to be concerned about if you have good intentions. I will define good intentions: Good intentions means you are able to love each other enough to live peacefully. That is it. This is the only thing you need to be able to do to remain here on earth and blossom into your true-selves. I will give you further suggestions when you are ready.

A Simple Way to Gain the Power of God

From Jesus:
There is a special way to connect with Me that is rarely done. It is a simple 'pretend' game. Pretend I am watching you as much as you can; all the time if you can. You will think much less. You will feel more peaceful. In time, you will be able accomplish more by doing less – much more. You will have much more support from Me. You will gain the power of having Me in your life.

The reason for this is that when you think of Me, you are silently telling the Source of creation energy that you have Me by your side. This will bring more universal support than meditation, visualizing exercises, applying any learned knowledge or having any other connection with any human or spiritual being.

I am the power, I am the way, I am the life, I am pure love. There is no source of power that does not go through Me. Go to Me directly. See Me with you, watching you, loving you. Give Me your attention. Ask Me to take care of everything you need and just watch Me watching you throughout your day.

Can someone that is non-Christian benefit from doing this?
Yes. Your beliefs are of no relevance. I am with all equally. I love all equally. I am that universal energy of love, compassion and non-judgment. It is *you* who are not with *Me*; it is *your* awareness that is not with Me.

How can you love all equally? That sounds hard to understand. Don't You love mean or cruel people even a little less than kind, loving people?
Not an ounce less. Love needs not a reason to love. Real love, unconditional love, does not see that which is not loving. There is no

such thing. When you see someone as unlovable, it is because you see yourself as unlovable in some way. Anything less than loving is a figment of your imagination.

I don't really understand that. There are people in this world that are mean and cruel and do bad things; even horrible things that hurt others. What they do is very real.
If you were fully aware of the love that you are, as I am, you would not be affected by anything but love. You would realize the unloving actions of others are not real.

But, isn't the pain they cause to others very real?
Yes, it feels real now. But it is not real, no. Think of what happens when you awaken in the morning from a dream of conflict or suffering. You think something like: "Oh, it was only a dream. It wasn't real. It's over now. Thank God it wasn't real. It was only a dream". It is like this when you wake up to the awareness of God. You will then understand.

I don't understand how you can say that pain is not real. It is very real to us.
Yes, I know. That is why I am communicating to you and asking you to share My messages. This is why I gave you this suggestion. If you want freedom from all suffering you have to develop more awareness of the love that you are; this is your true nature. Intentionally connecting to Me directly, is the easiest and fastest way to achieve this awareness.

Healing Principles Direct from Spirit

The following healing principles were received directly from spirit. Many are familiar with Jesus, Mother Mary, Mahavatar Babaji and Buddha. Other conversations included here are from an angel and the deceased family members of my friend, Mette Bergmann.

Jesus
What would you like to say about healing?
Healing is an unnecessary process. I would like to discuss an ideal way to heal all aspects of who you are so you can reach a place where you will never again need healing.

Let's start with the physical. Physical healing occurs to a limited degree when using physical modalities. It is good to be mindful of how to properly take care of your physical body. But, a much larger part of the creation of physical illness is a result of how healthy and balanced you are mentally, emotionally and spiritually.

All true healing comes from Me, from love energy. The spirit of who you are is My love energy. Love energy heals everything at the same time. So, rather than focus on divided sections of what needs to be healed, such as an imbalanced organ, a harmful emotion or a mental symptom, be more whole minded with healing and connect with Me – love energy that heals all simultaneously and more effectively than a mere fragment of who you are.

A loving heart is what heals all forms of imbalances: mental, emotional, physical and spiritual. You may address a symptom and experience improvement for a time, but why not focus on the source of *all* symptoms? This is an unhealed heart.

A heart in need of healing forms imbalances on all levels. Only the love that you are can heal your heart. Love heals the source of all imbalances which is the presence of fear. This is done by becoming more aware of the love that you are. Your true nature – LOVE - already exists perfectly. If you do not know this, it is because fears block your awareness of your true-self.

How do you remove fears?
By recognizing them.

Fear manifests into all forms of dysfunction within your being and universe. Some of you already know this, yet the fear still remains. So, becoming aware of your fears is the first step to truly healing anything.

"Babaji's Work" specializes in conquering the ego [the cause of all problems] more effectively, quickly and easily than anything else. His work consists of easily identifying your unhealed pains and the underlying fears that caused them.

When you have identified a particular fear, it is healed by giving it your full attention and acceptance. You continue to do this with each fear you have identified until they are all gone. Then you will be at the one pain you have left to heal – the pain from the perceived loss of God which occurs at birth. Feel this pain and you will then be set free.

This brings not only mental, emotional and physical balance but also spiritual expansion, which is the growth of the love energy that you are. This is your soul. When your heart and spirit are fully expanded, which occurs when you are freed from all fear, you become fully aware of who you really are – pure love energy - God.

Babaji's Work is the narrow path to becoming free of all pain, separation and fear. Doing Babaji's Work regularly will free you from attracting all forms of dysfunction with the purpose of healing your pain.

Mahavatar Babaji
What would you like to tell people about healing?
Anything that needs healing needs your acknowledgment, compassion and validation. It needs to be felt fully. Feel your pain. Try to feel your pain. Ignore nothing. Then surrender your pain to Christ. This is healing.

Mother Mary
What would you say about healing?
Healing can only occur when you succumb to what causes a need to heal – your ego's beliefs, pain and fear. Many of you continue to create ongoing imbalances in your life in numerous ways; otherwise referred to as "problems". You create them in your experiences.

> *You create problems because you have a need to heal something.*

My Son's love is all you need to heal anything. So, experience my Son's love by learning and practicing what He teaches.

> *You will know you are practicing His teachings if they make you feel more loving to yourself and to others.*

Are you feeling happier, more peaceful, more inner joy with an automatic desire to share that peace and joy with others? If so, you are on the right path to healing. If you feel a level of "emptiness" inside, as though something is missing, it is a result of being disconnected from my Son. My Son is your eternal self. Help others heal if you want to be healed. This will connect you to my Son quicker than anything.

Buddha
What would you like to say about healing?
Healing has been needed for millions of years. Eventually, after the beginning of human existence, people became affected by the state

of ignorance they were in and began to digress spiritually. The force of digressing spiritually has been progressing for millions of years.

The time has come on earth where you must heal spiritually. You must focus on evolving spiritually. There are many ways to do this. A few are:

- Feel your uncomfortable feelings. Become comfortable with feeling those uncomfortable feelings. If you avoid such feelings, they will strengthen. Negative emotions are a part of being human, whether you are enlightened or not. Get comfortable with them.
- Learn how to forgive yourself for not being what you think is more perfect. Realize you will never live up to your ego's expectations. Nor will anyone else.
- Become loving, compassionate and forgiving to yourself and others by doing good deeds for others. Help others be healthier and happier. If it is a struggle to forgive yourself or anyone else, take action to help improve the lives of others. This will quickly dissolve your judgment and guilt.
- Find peace. Be peaceful. Feeling peaceful comes from having a still mind. Meditate every day. Gain control of your insane, continuous thinking.

An angel who calls himself "a healing angel"
Be good to yourself. Be good to others. This means to be loving, kind and compassionate to yourself and others. Forgiveness is the key to healing. If you are beating yourself or others over the head with a hammer for not being better, you will get more sickness in various ways; sick minded, sick hearted, sick physically, sick habits, sick finances, sick relationships, sick life.

Edith (Mette's deceased mother)
Edith died after a long and arduous battle with cancer. She was also coping with the terminal illness of her adult son, Claus.

My definition of being healed is not to even need to be healed in the first place. Begin by feeling at peace. No matter what is going on in your life, be at peace. Otherwise you will need to experience great ills.

If you are not at peace you harbor and store stress energy within your body's cells. In time, physical disease will manifest. It is much easier to prevent the disease than to deal with it after it has formed.

All you need to know is to be at peace with your life. If something causes you unease, fix it. If you cannot fix it because it is out of your control, accept it. That is the key to healing anything.

How can you say "just accept it"? What would you say about your child dying? In truth, it is unacceptable.
You say to yourself something like this: "I am going to miss my child greatly. I am heartbroken my child is dying. We will be together again. And for now, I will accept what is in my life as it is." If you must face an unwanted experience, accept it, so you can have peace through it. It is that simple.

Claus (Mette's deceased brother)
Claus was a middle-aged man who suffered greatly with a brain tumor before his death. According to Mette, he coped with a domineering spouse for all of his married life.

What do you have to say about healing?
Do not put up with anybody's crap. That will make you sicker than anything else. Do not be a doormat, do not be a peon, do not be a layover. If you let others mistreat you, this is a powerful form of self-deceit. You deny yourself goodness, kindness, love, anything good if you are letting people treat you poorly. Find a way to muster the courage if that is what it takes. Do not allow anyone to mistreat you. If you cannot work it out civilly with that person, turn the other way and get them out of your life.

I can tell you that if you support goodness for yourself, you will get goodness. If you allow mistreatment from others, you will get mistreatment from others and you will become sick in one way or another in time.

Asta (Mette's deceased step-mother)
In an earlier conversation with Asta, she said that she struggled greatly with low self-esteem her whole life and eventually it developed into a variety of debilitating physical conditions such as blindness, severely crooked fingers, amputated toes and later the amputation of both legs.

What is the first thing that comes to your mind about healing? Can you share some wisdom?
A healthy mind makes a healthy body and spirit. An unhealthy mind makes an unhealthy body and spirit. Having a healthy mind is not always so easy because of how we are typically conditioned to think. But, if you are able to love who you are, that is all you need to be healthy minded and healthy in body and spirit.

If you have problems loving who you are, you are going to have problems with everything else. I could tell you stories for eternity, but it all boils down to being able to love who you are.

Can you give an example?
Are you feeling good enough? If not, you do not love yourself as you are. I suggest asking yourself on a regular basis if you are happy with you, your life, who you are married to or who you are with or the friends in your life or where you are working. If you get a "no", you need to make a change.

Accepting unhappy circumstances because you do not even think about being able to achieve more, makes for deterioration on all levels of your being. You start going in that direction unknowingly and it is unlikely that you will ever turn it around. This makes one bad thing after another.

You get what you expect to get in your life. Expect little, you get little; expect goodness, you get goodness. All of this boils down to how much you love yourself. If you really love yourself you will not accept less than what is fantastic.

What if I don't really know how to love myself? How does someone learn how to love themselves more?
It is not something that one can learn overnight. You need to achieve a higher level of awareness and a more healed heart.

What exactly do you mean by achieving a higher level of awareness?
Increase your awareness of love. Love more.

But, Mette told me you were always one of the most kind, loving and giving people that she ever knew. So, I am confused by this. Could you please explain further?
I'm glad you asked, because this is the most important thing to know – **how** to love rightly. If you sacrifice loving yourself, sacrifice being good to yourself in an effort to care for others, you will create illness. It is just a matter of time. Your life becomes strained and you become drained. You may like to feel noble and altruistic by giving at the expense of your own peace and well-being, but this is not true love. Learn to love others in a healthy way, which includes loving yourself along the way.

I did not know how to love myself and what it meant to love others by being my true-self. I had the unconscious belief that I had to keep *doing* for others and neglect myself for the sake of others in order feel lovable. I did not feel worthy of being loved simply by *being* myself. I sacrificed my personal desires, goals and pleasures and also my health, by taking better care of others than myself. I put myself last. I was exhausted every day of my life, living to please others.

Jorgen (Mette's deceased father)
Mette describes Jorgen as having been a very positive, optimistic man who didn't take life too seriously. He had a tendency to focus on solutions rather than problems throughout life and he had a good sense of humor.

Do you have any advice about healing?
I am no expert but I can say that being good to yourself is the most important thing, probably, to have and maintain good health. If you are not good to yourself, you decline.

How was it that your health was so good when you smoked like a chimney and drank like a fish all your life? How was it that you were never sick?
I was a happy man. Yes, look how I was as a happy man. It was a pretty good life actually. Be as good to yourself as you can. Be as happy as you can and you'll be a superman.

Earth Devolving

From Jesus:
Earth has been devolving a long time, for millions of years. When humans first came into existence they were aware; fully aware. Human beings gradually came to identify with ego. Ever so gradually, they came to believe they were separate. This belief in separation created fear and their fear has been progressing ever since. "They" are you. You are at a unique time now; a time when this continuation of digressing has almost come to a halt.

Planet earth is also a being much like you; a different being, but a being nonetheless. Planet earth will not allow you to continue your backward momentum – not on earth anyway. Earth is changing the energy in its atmosphere to a higher frequency; a higher vibration. So, only people with a higher vibration of energy will be able to remain. Earth is being destroyed and it is now in 'survival mode'. Earth is trying to protect itself as do all beings. All beings have an 'immune system' and the instinct to survive.

Scientists know that everything is energy; living, moving, always changing energy. This is not a new concept. Yet, many of you do not think of earth or your body's selves in this way. This makes you vulnerable; very vulnerable.

Many of you have been somewhat brainwashed and mostly by religions. This has kept you stuck from growing spiritually. I am returning to earth a second time in the form of direct communication through Connie and others to help you become willing to evolve to a higher level of awareness, a higher level of understanding, a higher level of energy vibration. This means a higher level of loving. In other words, I am here to help save you a second time from self-destruction. I am not going to rise from my grave in the form of my previous body or in another physical body, as some of you may be expecting.

Please know I am *always* with each of you. I am always *within* each of you. But you can only feel Me - or experience and know Me - by *giving* your love to yourselves and others; *expressing* your love to yourselves and others. I *am* the love that you are expressing.

You expand your awareness of Me by expanding your heart. This is done by extending your love. This is how to 'have' Me in your life. Give love. Give is a word of action. You need to put the love energy that you already have, which is Me, into action to bring it into your awareness; to experience it; to feel it and to cultivate more of it.

I am here to help you make the transition from ego identification to full awareness of your spirit self. This may be called enlightenment or God realization as you become aware of your Source through the direct experience of your Creator, your Higher Power.

God will never be fully understood by the mind only. Never. God is an experience, not a belief system.

Believe whatever you want to believe, but grow spiritually. Expand your heart. A lot of chaos is coming to earth very soon in different forms. All of it comes from man's actions, but some forms of chaos will be intentional and some will not be intentional; what you may call natural disasters.

Natural disasters occur because humans are unbalancing the energy of the earth. All energy *you feel* (emotions), emanates out into earth's atmosphere. This energy you give out, affects everyone, including earth. People get physically sick because the energy within their being (body) is out of balance. When the energy on earth gets imbalanced, it also gets 'sick', which results in the form of natural disasters. They do not occur by mistake or happenchance.

> **Sickness tells you something is wrong.**
> **Sickness develops because you do not effectively deal**
> **with your negative emotions as they arise.**

This leads to energy imbalances on all levels in your universe; sickness to yourselves, to animals, to wildlife, to earth. You have come to believe that sickness is simply a part of life. I tell you it is not "normal" for humans, wildlife or earth to 'get sick'.

What can you do that is helpful to yourself, to all beings on earth and to earth itself? You can deliberately choose to be more loving, caring and kind. I will tell you exactly how to be more loving, caring and kind. Think of the needs of others. Think of what might be helpful to another. Expand your ever-day attention beyond your immediate family and friends to also include neighbors, your community and whoever may cross your path. Begin to notice others as an opportunity for serving and realize this is also an opportunity to grow your love. It can be as simple as a smile, a sincere compliment, picking up a piece of litter or acknowledging appreciation.

Start living to serve your Creator rather than serving only yourselves. You do this by serving others in a balanced and rewarding way. Find a way to help others that is also pleasing to you. In addition to random acts of kindness, be an active channel and find ways to contribute regularly. Put into action your own particular talents that make you feel more useful or fulfilled. This also naturally increases your feelings of gratitude.

Find your own way to help one another that does not feel as a sacrifice nor feed resentment. Rather, choose to do that which increases your inner joy and sense of purpose. If you do nothing but live each day with alertness to opportunities for assisting others, you expand your heart and gain the ability to feel more love. You will grow spiritually.

Also, understand that as you use judgments against others for being different, for looking, thinking, talking or believing differently than you, you become less happy, less peaceful, less loving. Through judging yourselves and others you have been creating more and more separation and fear. You are getting back what you have given out. Know there is never an exception to this law of creation. Whatever you give out will eventually come back to you – be it called 'good' or 'bad'. Take responsibility and do not feel like a victim. No one is ever a victim. If you think you have been 'victimized', it is because you needed the experience to learn something. It is always a deeper level of love that you really need. I urge you to let go of your mistaken need to change others and change yourself instead. It is time to grow up. Do not hoard your love anymore. Please come to Me.

Mahatma Gandhi Speaks on Kindness

It is nice to be able to communicate to you now. This is a rare celebration. There is much to be said and I will be very happy if you would give my words to as many people as you can as soon as possible. I will not get into the challenging times ahead. You have heard enough about that, and I am more of one to focus on the good in any situation.

An inside knowledge this will be; from a source that knows what is going on inside, not just surface levels. You already know what is soon coming ahead in the world. A need for peace, mother earth is at. Earth's energy is no longer going to be able to tolerate all the negative energy that is given to it. And, you already know what you need to do to continue thriving and to help other people continue to thrive also. What I would like to say is a lot about kindness and how kindness is going to be able to win the war.

Kindness is the same as peacefulness and is the same as love and the same as compassion and the same as tolerance. This is completely lost in society. Kindness means to be able to be happy and being happy means being kind to yourself. Not busy, busy, busy. Not pushing, pushing, pushing. Not damning, damning, damning. And not expecting happiness to begin with.

The first goal for everyone is being happy with your selves. You cannot be good to others if you are not happy. So, this is what I would like to talk about. Happiness includes nothing that most people think it does. It does not include anything in the physical existence. Happiness does not come from anything in the physical; good physical health, good physical location of living, good people and circumstances in your life, good material things.

> *Happiness develops when your soul is growing.*
> *When your spirit is growing, happiness comes automatically.*

I will tell you my personal opinion about what makes the spirit grow better than anything: Being happy. Happiness is dependent on how you feel about yourself. So, how do you feel? If you feel good about yourself, you do good things. You do good things. Good things for yourself, good things for others. Everyone knows what is good and not good. It is not good to abuse yourself or others, be mean to yourself or others or hard on yourself or others. Being kind to yourself first brings being kind to others.

Would you further explain how to be kind to ourselves?
Doing good things. What do you want to do that is good? Figure out what good things you want to do for yourself and for others. This will bring happiness and happiness makes the spirit grow. And that is the only thing you need to know… "What good things do I want to do for myself and others today"? Then, do them!

Surrendering
Connie Asks; Jesus Answers

You suggest surrendering our needs to You. Why? What is the value of surrendering and how do we do it?
When you surrender something to Me - a need, a solution, a desire, I am able to put power behind it; power behind what you surrender to Me. My power to create is unlimited and until you develop the full power to create as I do, giving it to Me enables Me to support your goal.

There is a special and miraculous energy shift that takes place when you intentionally surrender your will to Me. A force begins to create a lot of movement – literal movement. Creation energy is behind this force. Creation energy starts moving to coordinate specific outcomes on earth in ways that will physically manifest in your life.

The most important thing to know about surrender is to release it. Once you have consciously surrendered to Me, forget about it. Consider it done. Release any worry, fear, doubt and feelings of unworthiness or despair. Negative emotions attached to what you have surrendered, literally reverses the progress of energy moving to support your goal.

If you experience positive feelings connected to your desire such as joy, peace, gratitude and the trust that all is well, your energy will then combine with My energy and that is when miracles occur. This is when a mountain can be moved to the sea. Your goal is to surrender your need to Me and detach yourself from it, as if you know without any doubt, that I will bring it to you; this, or something better. In order to do this you need to develop trust in Me. Trust in Me will never fail you - never.

When you become adept at learning how to surrender, you become free from suffering, free of fear. Surrendering is very simple yet hard to accomplish without feeling more love. It is the connection to My love that enables you to surrender with less effort.

Why do I feel a reluctance to let go and surrender fully? I seem unable to fully detach myself from caring about the outcome of a desire.
The reason you are not surrendering in the first place is because you have forgotten who you are. You are not connected with Me, with the love that you are. In your awareness, this creates fear and that fear is your ego. And, your ego always likes to feel that it is in control. It wants you to be ego-identified, not God-identified.

> Know that anything which creates fear
> or separation comes from the ego.
> Anything unifying or loving comes from God.

If you surrender control to God, you are putting God in charge of your life rather than your ego. When you are identified with the ego you will resist anything and everything. That is its nature; resistance to whatever is. Should you get everything you want, the ego will then cause you to worry about losing it. Then, ego will also search for something more to want. It is a never-ending story. There is no end to the dissatisfaction of the ego. It never stops wanting. It is a total absence of peace.

Begin loving more and you will start taming the ego's predominance in your life. Your love will automatically start replacing it. The only way to be able to surrender fully is to be fully identified with Me. The qualities you experience that come from Me (love) are peace, joy, happiness, compassion, trust, gratitude, humility and fullness. So create a new habit by consciously surrendering and re-surrendering as needed.

I have strong desires that remain unfulfilled. I know others that do also. We think we surrender. We think we asked you appropriately and believed to the point of expectation. Why do we sometimes not get what we want? One client of mine is unable to have children that she desperately wants. Why?
The client you are speaking of could have children if she were not so stuck in her beliefs. She is not open to hearing and following specific guidance she has been given. In her case, that is all she needs to conceive a child. I think you are asking about certain times when a desire is not meant to be achieved because it is not for their highest good.

Yes, I am asking that.
To surrender includes being able to accept that you may not get your desire. That is surrendering. You trust and know that if you do not get it, it would not have been in your best interest to receive it. Surrender, surrender, surrender. You will have to be able to surrender everything and anything your ego is resisting in order to gain the peace of God.

So, I am hearing that to achieve our desires, we surrender them to God with detachment from the outcome of those desires. The detachment is achieved through trusting in God. Trusting in God is also trusting in the process, right?
Yes, you must trust in Me to be able to fully surrender. This is what enables you to surrender. Also, you must know Me in order to trust in Me. How do you get to know Me? By extending your love, you experience more of Me. This is how to know Me.

THE VALUE OF PRAYER AND A DEEPER KNOWLEDGE OF HOW TO PRAY
Connie Asks; Jesus Answers

What is the Value in Prayer and How Should We Pray?

Prayer has been misunderstood for ages, so I am glad you asked. Prayer is meant to be for one reason and one reason only; to express your gratitude to our Father, our Creator. You are meant to be living your lives in peace, harmony and ecstatic joy, so much so that you naturally want to express your gratitude for life. Life, lived rightly, is a living prayer.

However, over time, people identified with ego and became fearful. Gratitude began to gradually decrease. In time, prayer turned into desperate cries for help. Since you are presently at a state of awareness that includes mostly fear, it is 'OK' to pray from a place of feeling you need help. But, the best way to pray for help, is to pray absolutely. By that I mean, with absolute power – with My power.

Many people think the more they cry and plead, the more they will be given an advantage. This is not correct. Some think that if taking the position of a beggar, they will be more heard. This is untrue. Remember that I said fear disconnects you from Me – Me who is the love and power in you? And, that the only thing separating you from fully experiencing My love and power is your fear? So, notice that if you feel like a beggar, you are filled with fear. When you do so, you place yourself at a greater distance from Me.

Your goal is to be in alignment with Me, so you need to feel more as I do. The qualities you need to feel to gain absolute power with your prayer requests are: love, compassion, non-judgment, joy, peace, gratitude, humility and trust. If you feel these qualities fully, you will have the full power of *You* – through Me – because you are feeling My qualities; the qualities that come from pure love.

If you feel weak you are limiting your power. If you feel helpless, you are limiting your power. Be the powerful, loving force you are *through* Me. "Through Me" means by being like Me - all loving, all compassionate and all non-judgmental - through feeling the qualities of love, My love, your love, our Father's love. Until you are fully aware of the love that you are and the power that goes with it, give your prayer request to Me. Surrender it to Me with trust and faith and know that I am God.

Knowing I am God means you recognize I am the power behind the Source of creation. If you feel separate from that (Me), you are. Not in truth, but in *your version* of reality. Aim to have the desire and willingness to be more like Me. The more loving, compassionate and non-judgmental you are, the more peaceful, joyful, happy, grateful, humble and trusting you will be. When you feel these qualities fully, as I do, you have all the power to create as I do. Your desires will be spontaneously manifested without even the need to ask.

So, when you ask Me to create something for you, do it while feeling gratitude for what you presently have and with confidence and faith *in Me*. Trust that I will bring it to you and that if I do not, it is because it would *not* have helped you. You are also developing humility simply by giving it to Me; by surrendering it to Me to create for you. Until you fully know the love you are and the power you have, you need to go through Me to realize it. You need to adopt the qualities that I am.

If you presently feel and believe you are limited, you cannot know you are unlimited. You cannot trust in yourself as being all powerful. If you are at this state of awareness you can more easily trust in Me. You can have more faith in Me. Use Me as the catalyst I came to earth to be for you. I am the missing link to remembering who you really are – all loving, all powerful and at one with all. Trust in Me until you can trust in yourself.

What about certain times of hardship such as losing a job, a way of life or even a loved one? How can someone pray during a time like this without feeling fearful, helpless and desperate, and as a beggar?

Through surrender. If you are fearful you are resisting the situation, not accepting it. If you were truly surrendering the situation to Me, you would trust and know that you and all involved will be enhanced from whatever the outcome of the situation. God does not make mistakes. Trust this. Know this without any doubt. If you did know this, you would not be praying with fear even during a challenging situation. It is your fear that makes it seem so challenging in the first place. Pray for what you want, but pray without fear. This is what enables Me to create miracles for you.

Please know that to have fear is to have more unhealed pain. Doing *"Babaji's Work"* will heal your suppressed pain. You will learn to feel the pain with acceptance which will result in the healing of it. This process prevents the need for you to undergo an actual painful learning experience.

Spiritual evolving is becoming more love and less fear.
This is what is needed to be fully
with Me in your awareness;
To remember that you are God as much as I am.

There are some times in life I do not understand why You do not seem to be supporting what I consider a good desire of mine. For example, I very much wanted to have children. I feel I would have been a wonderful mother. Having a child would have enabled me to love more. But, You did not give me this opportunity that I prayed for. Why? How could NOT having a family help me love more and recognize my "true self" more? This made no sense to me for a long time and used to make me feel angry, resentful, confused, disheartened and even betrayed by You.

The answer is because if you had a child, you would have put your time, energy and devotion to your child, rather than directly to Me in the way that you have. There is nothing 'wrong' with wanting and having a child. But, it is your time to come to Me, not to a child. It is your time to reach enlightenment. In your case, having a child would have significantly delayed reaching fullness, self-realization, enlightenment. You will not always understand everything. You need to learn how to accept not knowing or not understanding. Surrender is the only way to make peace with an unwanted situation, which often includes not understanding why you are not getting what you desire. Please – always trust in Me and know I am God. Know I will never steer you wrong.

What form of prayer is the best way to commune with You? That is, to connect with You and develop a closer personal relationship with You?
I want this from you more than anything; your time and attention; your heart, your love, your devotion, especially in a time of quietude. When you are not distracted and you are praying to feel closer to Me, you are filling my heart with more of your love – literally. As you continue to connect with Me in this intentional way, you are able to feel more and more of the presence of My Spirit, My love, My peace, My all-knowingness (referred to as your intuition), My compassion, forgiveness, inner joy, trust and gratitude. Some of you call this the Holy Spirit.

Please talk to Me as much as you can. Tell Me how you feel, what you need, what you fear, what you appreciate. Tell me what you are grateful for. We gain much more progress unifying (or merging) our spirits together from these times of communing. The more you commune with Me, the more the presence of My spirit infuses into your being and your consciousness. Also, pray for others. Pray for others to have what you desire for yourself. Pray for what you feel they need. Pray for others to come closer to Me.

Here is a 'gift' to help you come to Me: When you go to sleep at night, think of Me a few moments first. The most important thing to feel at this time is **My** love for **you**. Have the specific intention of feeling the love I have for you. Imagine Me watching you lying down, loving you, adoring you, cherishing you. I love every unique aspect of you more than you can imagine. But, imagine this a few moments before going to sleep. Feel how much you are loved. Doing this will connect us more when you sleep. What you feel when you go to sleep stays with you during your sleep. If you do this, you will be communing with Me while you sleep.

Jesus Defines Self-Forgiveness

I was born in Bethlehem. I was raised by my mother and father until the age of two. I was then placed in the care of others. I could not stay within harm's way. People were starting to notice I was different.

How were you different?
I was talking and saying riddles that were complex. It became obvious I was not a 'usual' baby. My parents knew I would be considered a threat, so they gave me to a loving family that lived away from being noticed.

Who and where was this family?
They were friends of my parents. My parents would come visit me when they could for we lived a day's journey away in a more secluded location.

What were the riddles that you were saying?
I was speaking in tongues – different languages. I was also starting to shine a light from my heart chakra. It was noticeable to the human eye.

What were you saying in different languages?
I was just speaking different languages. I was becoming one with all languages. All knowingness was beginning to develop.

What were you saying in the riddles?
Words that began with AUM or AMEN, then a sequence of other words that came to me naturally; words that an enlightened person becomes aware of and may verbalize. Saying these groups of words vibrates stillness into your being.

Do the words have any meaning?
Yes. They call our heavenly Father to us.

How? Can you explain more?
Saying them draws Him near because you are aligning yourself with His presence. He is a presence that is absolute stillness. If you align your being more in tune with His presence, you draw more of Him into you.

Was it like chanting?
Yes.

Why did you begin with the word AUM or AMEN?
It is the sound of creation.

I thought that was the word "OM"?
It is accurately pronounced AUM, as in AMEN. As I was born the son of God for the sole purpose of saving the human race from self-destruction, I became fully enlightened – "all" again at the age of ten. My purpose was to start helping people learn how to love. I became fully aware of my purpose and began teaching the word of God – truth, love, forgiveness, forgiveness being on the forefront. Forgiveness leads to all of love's qualities. I then became a teacher, teaching to love and not to fear.

I had to leave all I knew at the age of fifteen. I had to wait for God to bring people to a place of willingness for Me and My teachings. I want to talk about this time I had in solitude while waiting. This time felt like a few moments. It was actually many years. I transcended time and space here and this is what I want to talk about.

What do you mean by "transcended time and space"?
I dissolved time and space. I went beyond time and space. The presence of God is timeless. I was in a state of ecstasy every moment. I was at one with God and all, yet still in a human body. I want to describe what this was like and how I was able to forgive all fear qualities all of you had created. I did not ignore them – all the fear qualities that I personally felt and experienced from each and every one of you. I accepted feeling them fully. I absorbed them fully. One

by one by one, I fully felt all the fear that each of you had developed by forgetting the truth of who you are.

I did this with ease and grace because I mastered forgiveness. I mastered acceptance. I mastered honoring your fear. One by one by one, I faced your self-created fear. When I dissolved the force behind your fear, you were all ready for Me. You were ready to learn the difference between the part of you that is not real and the part of you that is.

This is when I began exposing myself publicly to teach this truth. Yet, I could not force it upon you. You had to be willing to accept it. Patience was then a great challenge for Me and I wore a heavy garment on my back until the moment My body died.

I wanted for you all to know the fullness of life that was available for you now. That began My pain; excruciating pain. I had to learn how to transcend all my love for you, which was a constant challenge. I wanted to give you what was yours to receive, but you had to become willing to accept it.

The day I died on My cross was the moment I accepted your denial of Me and of our Father. This was a world-changing moment for you all. My forgiveness was not accepted and you chose to remain in need of forgiveness for yourselves, from yourselves.

All of you are here again at a similar time. Instead of needing My forgiveness, you need your own forgiveness. Many of you will reject forgiving yourselves just as you rejected My forgiveness. I want you to understand what self-forgiveness means.

Self-forgiveness is loving yourself enough To free yourself from all the fear you created.

You could have done this before I died because I forgave you first. I created the forgiveness that was needed to be reborn. Being reborn means becoming free from all your fear. If you do not forgive yourselves as I already have, another world changing event will take place.

A new earth is going to be formed. An earth that becomes free from all fear. Many of you are at the same place you were when I was a human on earth as Jesus Christ. You have a choice to make; love or fear. Should you choose fear, you will never again be on this earth.

You will be relocated to another planet that is more dark and barren. It is nearly void of life as you know it. It will deepen your experience of fear. This will enable you to succumb to it. Succumb to it now – while you are still here on earth. How do you succumb to it? You do *"Babaji's Work"*. You do what I did with your fear. You give it your full attention. You honor it. You accept it. You give it what it needs – your attention; your allowance. You do not resist it. This will dissolve its existence. You will move and grow beyond your fear.

Know that you cannot hide from this forever. This is a time in your evolution to dissolve your fear. God will bring you what you need to do this. Do it here on earth, not on the after earth planet. Do Babaji's work once daily (or more if desired). This will be allowing your fear to be felt, to be honored, to be dissolved. You will be willing to forgive your fear if you are willing to do *"Babaji's Work"*. Your willingness to forgive your fear is again needed to continue on earth. Please do not again choose resistance.

Forgiveness means to allow whatever is. When you accept whatever is, you have no more judgment about it. Then, it needs no forgiveness, because you are fully allowing it to be.

You said a light was shining from your heart chakra. What was that and why was it happening?
It is love energy. When you reach a more enlightened state, more love energy is in your heart. In time it becomes so powerful that a light begins to shine from it.

How were you able to contain so much love energy in your heart?
I let the ego's identity be as it was without giving it power. I did not resist it. I let it be its fearful self. Then love energy soared within, extremely rapidly. I continued to accept our Father's love into My heart.

Is our Father, our Creator, love energy or just energy?
He is pure love energy as am I. But, when I was born into a physical body and physical existence, I too had an ego. It just needs to be permitted to exist without believing in it. If you believe in it, your perception of who you are (and all in your life) is now fear-based and separation-based. The longer you believe in it, the more it grows and the more powerful it becomes in your mind; the more attached to it you become.

> *Ego is only an illusion. But, if you believe in it,*
> *It then becomes reality to you; a*
> *distorted version of reality.*

Allow it to be the fear which it is and always will be. Simply do not believe this is all of who you are. See beyond the ego's identity by allowing it to be. You can only cross over to the other side of ego by fully accepting it. This requires courage.

How could you have that level of courage at the age of two?
I *noticed* my ego's fear. I let it be and therefore, I did not believe it was who I was. I remained non-identified with, non-attached to my ego's fear because I did not resist it. If you resist it, it is because you fear it. Your perception is already fear-based if you are resisting it. You are then identified with and controlled by your fear, which is your ego. Fear is now in your perception and your perception is your reality. I was aware of fear being there and I chose to allow the fear to be, not resist it.

I've been trying to "surrender my ego" for many years. I am still not near to accomplishing that. Why?
You are near to accomplishing that. If you were doing *"Babaji's Work"* daily as Babaji and I have suggested, you would be self-realized already. You would realize and therefore experience your true self's identity, which is all loving, all unifying and with no fear, no separation. Your ego still predominates in your awareness. Your perception is still ego-based, fear-based. Honor and allow the fear that remains by giving it your attention. Intentionally feel and heal the pain that remains. This is doing Babaji's work.

Connie Says: I really did not like hearing that because it is so true. Ouch!

HEAL EMOTIONAL PAIN WITH "BABAJI'S WORK"

From Jesus:
Mahavatar Babaji is a helper of Mine. He specializes in dissolving fear quickly. *"Babaji's Work"* is an effective method to identify those underlying fears that cause you ongoing pain from past and present experiences. Many have specific fears, yet do not recognize them because of unhealed emotional pain.

All pain must be healed if you would experience all fullness of life. Emotional pain comes from judgments which are caused by fears. Some fears you may recognize others you do not. Many of you are attached to believing in your ego's judgments. Your life is very limited if you perceive everyone and everything with fear-based, separation-resulting judgments. A limited life means living a life experiencing pain – with trials and tribulations. The source of your judgment is your fear. *"Babaji's Work"* gets you to the fear, the source of your pain. You bypass your judgment by doing *"Babaji's Work"*.

Staying stuck in your judgments will continue the creation of ongoing painful experiences. You are not consciously aware that you do this. You are not consciously aware that it is YOU who creates or attracts your unwanted experiences.

> **The whole purpose for the pain arising is to "grab your attention" to it, Giving you the opportunity to heal it.**

I define *"Babaji's Work"* as feeling your suppressed emotional pain. You are going to have to face it and feel it in order to accept it and heal it. Accepting it through surrender is the only way to heal it.

Avoid it, continue to fear it, and it will only grow and strengthen in time.

When you do *"Babaji's Work"* but once daily, you end the need to actually experience ongoing, painful events. Remember, the recurrence of attracting experiences that cause you painful emotions is for the purpose of surrendering your fear. Surrender the fear first. For with *"Babaji's Work"*, you will save lifetimes of unnecessary suffering.

> *Fear is the cause of all your suffering, not the person, circumstance or events, Which in your judgments, appear to be the cause.*

When you are in guilt, blame or shame or any form of pain, it is because you have a fear that needs to be acknowledged; allowed simply "to be" without judging it; fully felt and fully accepted. Then and only then are you free from it. Then and only then you will no more experience pain for the purpose of healing your fear.

I know who Mahavatar Babaji is but will you please explain his relationship with You?
Babaji and I are already one. But, Babaji will not be complete until each and every one of you are at one with us in *your* awareness. When all of you on earth are enlightened, Babaji will be complete. He has chosen a path to help you all accomplish this. Babaji loves and cares for all of you as much as I do. Between My love and power and his strength and courage, this will be done.

Why do we need Babaji's strength and courage? Don't You have enough?
I have many helpers. You will not understand this answer Connie, but Babaji created the strength and courage needed to fully accept My love and power. I created a deeper level of love and power on earth when I was in human form as Jesus. All of you on earth had

created a collectively strong force of fear. So much that you were all about to destroy yourselves. Such a time in near again. That is why I created Myself as a human being on earth. The human race needed to be saved from self-destruction. I made this possible for you from My existence on earth as Jesus Christ.

Many of you are still not freed from all your fears. But, I enabled you to have more time to accomplish this by dissolving *the force* of your fear. This is the time I confronted "Satan", as the Bible explains. Satan is a word for an energy force; a momentum of power or influence that consists of the entire collective fear energy in the world. That force became more powerful than the collective energy of your love. A different frequency was needed to balance the opposing fear energy. I helped you raise the collective consciousness of love on earth. Know that each and every one of you also affects the collective consciousness in the same way.

My love must be accepted by you to be received. This means you have to heal all your fear. Anything you fear must be healed to be fully at one with Me in Heaven. Heaven is a state of awareness that does not include fear.

After I left My physical body, I brought you Babaji. You were ready for a deeper level of strength and courage. This was needed for you to have the willingness to face your fear and accept My love. Babaji made this possible for you. Babaji gave this to you directly.

From Jesus:
Now for Babaji's Work. A sound (mantra) is used to help surface an underlying fear. Listen to the sound silently or out loud verbally. Repeat Babaji's mantra for about ten minutes. Saying this sound helps release deeply embedded fears.

Om Namah Shivaya
(Pronounced: om nah-mah shee-vi-ya)

Think about what most disturbs you right now. It will be a person, place, thing, event or circumstance. Are you angry at someone? Are you worried or struggling with uncertainty? Are you feeling shameful? Do you feel regret for a past action or inaction? Do you feel inadequate? Do you feel hatred toward yourself or someone else? Do you feel like a victim? Do you feel a sense of loss in some way? Do you feel sorrow, resentment, frustration, loneliness, guilt or even feel unloved and unlovable? The list could go on and on.

Select to identify one specific feeling at a time. Do not concern yourself with the issue or person who you think may have caused it. Simply identify the specific feeling. Now, think back to an earlier time in your life when you felt the same or similar feeling. Then, perhaps, an even earlier time until you remember your earliest memory of feeling that pain.

Allow yourself to notice the pain. Allow yourself to feel that pain. Just allow yourself to feel that pain as fully as you can. Know you are justified for having that pain. You are validated for feeling that pain. Watch with alertness so that you do not stay stuck in thinking about what happened to you. Just notice and intentionally feel the painful feeling that went with that experience.

The intensity of the feeling will reduce in time. It is a cycle that will 'spend' itself out, slightly or a lot. Stay with feeling the pain until you naturally feel a little lighter, a little brighter; until the intensity of the emotion fades. You will know when the cycle has completed for this session. Then, carry on with your day. That is it.

It is a simple practice. Give yourself about ten minutes (or more if desired) to get in touch with feeling your pain. Sometimes you will feel it intensely, other times mildly. This daily practice of identifying and feeling your fears will result in your automatic acceptance of them. This keeps you from staying stuck in the pain and *never getting to the cause of the pain.* The ego's delusional thinking is the root cause of all your pain and fears. *Babaji's Work* will get you out of this trap.

The Heart Technique

From Jesus:
The *"Heart Technique"**consists of five simple yet powerful methods of teaching that covers all aspects necessary to grow spiritually at a very rapid rate toward achieving full awareness (enlightenment). It is a 35 minute daily practice.

The Meditation Technique
This effortless meditation dissolves a common and deep-seated block that inhibits you from feeling your soul. When your mind is so busy with many unnecessary thoughts, you are prevented from experiencing your soul. As the nature of your soul is pure stillness and pure love, an over-active mind prevents you from feeling this. Therefore, an *effective* meditation is helpful to reduce activity of the mind.

There are many methods of meditation. This technique is unique and effective in that it directly calls your soul to awaken within. A specific sound (mantra) is used in a specific way that requires no focus, no concentration and no effort. It not only calms the mind and nervous system, it enlivens your soul in a way as no other sound can.

The Soul Awareness Technique
Becoming more aware of your soul as it resides in your body is a primary goal toward enlightenment. Your heart and soul are one. Your soul is pure stillness, pure love. The more you become aware of your soul's presence, the more permanently established you become in contentment, peace, joy and present moment awareness. This is what leads to true everlasting peace and happiness. Developing these qualities increases the awareness of your true self - who you are behind the outer identity of the ego. Soul awareness can be achieved only through direct experience, not through learning anything from the mind.

The *"Soul Awareness Technique"* teaches you how to directly contact and experience your soul. You automatically bypass every blockage to awareness of your soul by giving it your attention and actually feeling and experiencing it. The soul is initially a feeling that requires your attention and awareness. In time, the feeling of it transforms into the being of it.

The Self-Forgiveness Technique
Unhealed emotional pain is another obstacle that prohibits you from feeling your heart and soul to its full potential. Where there is pain, there is underlying fear - fear that you are in some way, "not enough". This underlying fear develops into various forms of self-loathing, such as, guilt, shame, victimization, loneliness, inadequacy or resentment. The ego can also alter it into blame, where you reposition it from yourself onto someone else or some outer circumstance. It is all the same fear – just a different form. No matter what form the fear takes, it reaffirms and deepens the belief that you are not enough. These conditions develop because you are not aware of your soul. All forms of self-loathing must eventually become healed for you to become fully enlightened. They are an illusion. But until you become aware of these illusions, you identify with them unknowingly and so they remain.

The experience of true self-love requires self-forgiveness. The *"Self-forgiveness Technique"* gives you what no one else can – *no one but you*. This technique is a remarkably simple and effective way to recognize and forgive yourself for all those mind-made illusions (beliefs) that prevent you from fully loving yourself.

Spontaneous Creation Technique
The *"Spontaneous Creation Technique"* opens a channel with the Source of creation. When you refine your energy vibration in this way it results in spontaneously creating a more fulfilling life.

All energy that makes up who you are in your physical existence is living, moving, dynamic energy. It is common knowledge that you all emanate an energy that can even be felt by others, such as loving, calming, happy, nervous, angry. The quality of that energy within your being attracts people, places and circumstances that *match your energy*. This is what you call the "law of attraction" and it becomes much more powerful with the practice of the "*Spontaneous Creation Technique*".

The Gratitude Technique
Where there is gratitude, there is a life-supportive force behind every thought you think, every feeling you feel and every action you take. It rushes to support someone with gratitude. The more gratitude you develop, the more this force follows you, quite literally, to support your dreams and desires. When your mind is calm and you have a higher soul awareness with a more open heart, your creative power is magnified greatly by feeling gratitude, even if only briefly.

*To learn more about the Heart Technique visit www.HeartTechnique.com

Why Jesus Gave Mette the Heart Technique

From Jesus:
I created the *"Heart Technique"* for Mette to teach others because it is greatly needed. All are reaching a time in your evolution where evolving spiritually is a must in order to continue to thrive. Earth's energy has been changing to a higher frequency. Mankind's energy has been changing to a lower frequency. This opposing and conflicting energy has been intensifying in strength and power, causing a wide variety of chaos and disorder on earth and increased stress in people's lives. Quality of life has been digressing as a result.

Your souls are yearning to be more realized and utilized. Your very being is striving to reach a foundation that is more in balance and harmony with divine order. This increasing feeling of unease, discontent or lack of joy is reaching an all-time high on earth. A 'breaking point' is near with earth's inability to withstand more friction-energy from humans.

I created the *"Heart Technique"* for Mette to teach to others, as she has both the intellectual understanding and the experiential knowledge necessary to discern precisely what disconnects people from their soul's peace, love and stillness.

Mette's dharmic path is that of a healer. She helps one heal the various conditions developed from ego-identification which slows the process of spiritual evolving. She has learned the difference between love and fear and the many different forms of fear that can unknowingly manifest in one's belief system. This is what keeps a person 'stuck' at a limited level of awareness. This is what inhibits spiritual growth and prevents one from experiencing more of who they really are.

These inhibiting, fear-based beliefs have become a world-wide epidemic and the world is now able to shift from the direction it has been moving for a very long time. The capacity for the creation of a 'new trend' is now possible. In fact, it is essential.

Please understand that no group, organization, religion or affiliation with any structured path will work to achieve enlightenment. The path to soul-awareness, is *not* a so-called 'correct' belief system. Enlightenment is revealed *only* through direct experience. Therefore, the *"Heart Technique"* does not challenge or interfere with anyone's culture, religion or belief system.

I have urged Mette to share the *"Heart Technique"* with others. Practicing it daily will rapidly expand your heart and soul.

Archangel Metatron Speaks on Pride

I am Metatron. I help people find God. Finding God has nothing to do with finding something. It has everything to do with uncovering the layers of beliefs that prevent you from knowing God. A most significant layer of delusion is pride.

Pride inhibits you from experiencing God. Pride believes it knows better than others. I refer to pride as an "it", not a "you". You are not pride, but you can have pride. When you have pride, you have deep guilt and shame. You have a severe case of the condition I call ignorance.

Ignorance is not knowing the experience of God. And when you think you know more than someone else does about God, you are going to be given a lot of loneliness. Loneliness is the most effective teacher to dissolve pride. I like helping people afflicted with pride. I am a master at dissolving pride.

When I am given a particular human to help, it is always because they have pride. I determine exactly what someone believes that is keeping them heavily stuck in the form of pride, for that is what prevents them from growing closer to experiencing God. I create experiences for them that will help them dissolve their pride. It is always a deeper experience of loneliness I bring to them.

Eventually, these people will feel so empty, they begin to open their hearts to those who they would not have before. Eventually, they will break down the barrier of judgments that is causing them to feel pride. Pride is a dangerous delusional belief. It creates strong separation to loving others. Loneliness is the 'tool' that helps dissolve pride should you remain unaware of it.

I'd like to help you make leaps and bounds forward toward dissolving your pride. If you have pride you have self-loathing. Everyone has self-loathing and it takes on many different forms. But, pride is particularly powerful in that it is a form of delusion that causes one to be closed-off, not open to learning something different.

> *If someone is not open to hearing something new,*
> *they are attached to their beliefs.*
> *They are unknowingly making a belief*
> *more important than love.*

Pride has the ability to keep one completely stagnant from expanding the quantity of love that you allow to flow through your heart.

I want to make clear that the *only* way to God is through the heart. And the only way to experience God fully is to have a heart that is fully open. So, now I want to help you understand whether or not you have pride. People that have pride do not realize it. So recognizing it in yourself will help get you out of it.

Please start by answering the following questions:

1. Do you think you are able to be closer to God than others because you have a different belief system?
2. Do you think you need to help others understand and believe what you do about God?
3. Do you ever get irritated when someone has a different concept of God than you?
4. Are you teaching about God from a set of rules?
5. Do you have the same beliefs about God and how to know Him that you had last year?

If you answered yes to any of these, then you have pride. And pride must be demolished to experience God fully. Pride and God oppose each other. Where there is pride, there is a lack of experiencing God's love.

The best way to dissolve pride is to have the willingness to let go of your attachment to your beliefs. Cut to the chase and choose to learn how to listen to someone else's beliefs with an open mind and open heart. You may or may not agree, but what you believe is irrelevant.

You will gain something valuable because you had the willingness and open-mindedness to go beyond your pride (attachment to your beliefs) in the process. This directly dissolves pride and you will again be moving closer to experiencing God more fully. Then you won't need me or a deeper experience of loneliness.

Can you give me a specific example of a belief system that can make someone feel they are closer to God than someone else who doesn't have the same belief system?
Yes. I will give you several. You used to be a vegetarian. You believed that being a vegetarian was better than being a meat eater. You judged meat eaters. You believed you were 'higher' than meat eaters. You even used to look down on meat eaters. You not only thought you were closer to God, you thought God favored you more because you were a vegetarian. This is pride.

You used to think the specific meditation program you learned and used to practice was better than other meditation programs. You thought you were closer to God than people that did not meditate or those who practiced a different meditation. You perceived them as an outsider. This is pride.

One of your Jewish friends thinks his faith is better than others. He thinks he is closer to God because of his belief system. This is pride.

Another one of your friends is Catholic. She thinks she is better than Jews and non-Catholic Christians. She believes she is more loved by God. She believes others are less loved by God. Non-Catholics threaten her beliefs. This is pride.

Your other friend is an Agnostic. He believes that not having a belief system about God (religion) is better than having any belief system. He thinks his belief system of not having a belief system is better. He thinks he knows better than they do. He thinks he is smarter and closer to the Creator than others. This is pride.

You used to have strong judgment toward alcoholics and drug addicts. You thought you were better than them. You judged them and looked down on them. This creates separation. This is pride.

But, I was always very kind and giving to homeless people on the street, including addicts. I often gave them money, meals, etc.
You had compassion for them, yes. A heart with compassion is a developed heart to a certain degree. But, in addition to your compassion was pride. You thought you were better than them.

Why People Tend to Resist Jesus

From Jesus:
Many people have a tendency to resist Me personally. Many have a misunderstanding of who I am and what I represent. I am here to help bring all people together and I understand that much of what you have learned about Me from others, including from books, is misinterpreted, distorted or completely incorrect.

Many of you associate Me with fear. Sometimes so much, that you deny My very existence as worthy of honoring. Some choose not to go near Me because they fear they will fail at ever being good enough for My supposedly high expectations. Some have so much fear associated with Me, they go in the opposite direction to avoid feeling their unworthiness and guilt. These people become strongly judgmental toward others in order to feel superior.

I want to impress the point that I do not judge, I do not criticize, I do not love you any less for being human. Until you are able to feel this way about yourselves, you are going to experience trials and tribulations.

When you realize what I do – that you are simply learning how to be human while gaining awareness of your true-self, you will realize that "imperfection" does not really exist. Imperfection is guilt, created from your ego, which is only an illusion. Accept that you are learning how to be your true-self while in a human body. Forgive yourself for not yet being fully aware of how perfect you already are. You cannot make mistakes. Learning is not a mistake.

You can perceive as I do if you have the willingness to let go of your guilt, which causes you to continue to judge yourselves (and others) negatively. I am here to help you accomplish this. Love yourselves and others as I do. And know that I do love you without limitations, conditions or exceptions.

Why do we experience trials and tribulations throughout life?
Your so-called "bad" or challenging experiences are teaching you what you fear. You need to become aware of what prevents you from developing awareness of God, your true nature, pure love. Your fears are the only thing that blocks you from knowing your true-self. When you reach full acceptance of what you fear, the fear is then gone. One by one, you will dissolve away your fears, quickly or slowly, depending on your level of willingness.

It is the gift of challenging circumstances which creates the opportunity to face and accept your fears, one by one. Practicing Babaji's work averts the need to experience the actual fear in your physical life. As you become aware of both your known and hidden fears, you can reach an acceptance of them. Surrender is to 'tool' that enables you to accept.

Surrendering your fears to Me will bring you more assistance toward reaching acceptance. Ask Me to help you with what you need. Maintain an open mind because if you are resisting something to begin with, you need the willing openness to something new. It is your beliefs (judgments) that keep you from knowing who you really are; from experiencing the presence of God – pure bliss consciousness, pure love, pure peace, pure stillness.

Jesus Defines the Presence of God

The presence of God is an energy. It is a feeling, a knowingness that is your soul. It is that non-physical part of you which is eternal. It is who you really are. It is who you always have been and always will be. I have referred to this as your "true-self". Your true-self is an energy; a presence that you feel and know is there. Your mind can never fully understand this part of who you are because it is not physical. The mind is limited and can only identify with the five physical senses, that is, what your physical body can touch, see, taste, hear and smell. This is how your mind knows what it knows.

Your true-self, your spirit-self or soul, is a presence that is always the same. It is unchanging pure love, pure peace, pure bliss and pure stillness. This is God. You are intended to live your life knowing this. There is nowhere in creation that God's energy does not exist and that includes you. You experience that un-formed, un-manifested energy through the all-knowing, unlimited nature of the soul. You can function in your physical body while at the same time feeling your soul's presence; while also having awareness of your soul's existence. This is enlightenment or God consciousness. This is living fullness of life.

> **Suffering is not possible when you are aware of the presence of who you are.**

I define suffering as perceiving and feeling any belief that comes from ego. Fear-based emotions are: sadness, guilt, anger, resentment, regret, dissatisfaction, insecurity, worry, inadequacy, separating judgments, loneliness, etc.

Many have lost touch with God's presence. The reason for this is you typically identify only from the mind through experiencing the five senses. This is what creates the ego; your physical identity. This is what leads to not knowing all of who you are.

Know that to exist in the physical world you must exist within limitations. You take on a physical form which identifies you as being "this" and not "that". Robert is not also David. A dog is not also a cat. The sun is not the moon. Every definition brings with it a limitation of what it is not. This is why God cannot be defined to any limited form. Again, there is nowhere God is not. God is unlimited, formless, eternal energy. God is also within you.

I recommend doing *"Babaji's Work"* and the *"Heart Technique"* daily. They work hand in hand to expand awareness of your true-self. This is the most beautiful, complete feeling you could ever imagine. *"Babaji's Work"* heals the ego by dissolving your fears and the *"Heart Technique"* heals by expanding awareness of your soul's presence. At this time, doing these two techniques daily is the most effective way to spiritually evolve.

I have been directly communicating to Connie for several years for the sole purpose of preparing the world to evolve quickly. It is time now for Connie and Mette to share the knowledge I have given them so you can begin living fullness of life. Please know that the fullness of life means the merging of both the joys from the external world ***and*** the blissful part of you that is real and not fleeting. Be with Me in your awareness and direct experience and choose to grow spiritually. Your conscious choice will make the transition to wholeness much quicker and easier.

I thank you in advance for your willingness to let go of your pain, your judgments and your fears. This is all that prevents you from knowing who you really are. Remember that all of you are already perfect and whole. You have only temporarily lost the awareness of your eternal self. You can and will transition to full awareness of your true-self again. Ask Me to help you through this process. I come to all that ask for Me – always.

JESUS DEFINES THE PROCESS OF CREATION

Creation is a hard thing to understand. The mind's understanding is such a limited existence. Creation started with absolute nothingness. There was nothingness for so long until this nothingness began to enliven. This nothingness was pure energy for a time. Enliven means this energy began to turn into awareness; awareness of Itself.

After more years than you can imagine, it started to become lonely. It, God, became such a powerful energy, it exploded and form was then born. The creation of form is a transition from timelessness to a sense of time; from nothingness to somethingness; from non-existence to existence; from non-physical matter to physical matter.

In exactly six days, earth and all existence of matter was formed. This includes all life-forms as you know it and many that you do not know. Different galaxies were created, including different life-forms in each galaxy. Different forms of energies were manifested – many different forms of energies. More than you could ever imagine.

Earth's galaxy is one of many. All in existence was perfect. Existence was completely neutral minded. It just was. Experience began. At first, experience started with non-judgment. There was no such thing. There was nothing to compare anything to. Gradually, judgment began by comparing a present experience to a past experience. At first, this comparing was not judged, but it progressed into judging the comparison. A false sense of reality began.

Beings became more aware of the process of judging than of the experience behind the judging. Your judgment became stronger and stronger until you lost complete awareness of the experience behind the judgment. Since judgment is not real and is only a perception, awareness of reality was lost. You could now know only your perception as reality.

If you were an actor playing a part on a stage and became so engulfed in the scene of the play for so long, you would eventually forget the existence of the actor's off-stage world. You would become so caught up in the drama of the play, you would forget it was only a play and you, the actor were only there to demonstrate your character's experiences from this perspective. This perspective is only one of many perspectives. Each and every person would have a different perspective of the scene on the stage. It becomes a mind-made illusory existence. You have forgotten who you are behind the veiled perception of your self-chosen roles.

For a time, this felt okay to you all. You were going along with it unknowingly; unaware. But, you started to notice a feeling of something missing – your true self – your soul – God. You did not know what this something missing was because you were aware of only the actor's stage. You had no more memory of life off the stage. Fear and emptiness strengthened over a long period of time. It has been intensifying ever since.

You all feel lost, afraid, incomplete and confused, but do not know how to let go of your mind-made illusory existence. You are stuck in an illusion. You are afraid to let go of the beliefs you have invested in for a long time. You would need to accept dying to realize the true you again. Your mind-made self (ego's identity) would have to acknowledge that all this time, its thoughts (beliefs) were not real. Your mind-made self does not want to become realized for then you would abandon it, preferring the God-realized part of who you are.

Your soul is the God-realized part of who you are that is pure love energy. I experienced love for Myself in the form (body) of Jesus Christ. I absorbed all the love you all had created and I dissolved the fear you created. You all chose to keep your own fear to yourselves. So, I took the fear given to earth, as earth did not refuse my blessing.

When you can no longer bear the existence you have created from your mind, you will choose to let go of it. And then you will be able to be your true self, who you really are, *while simultaneously experiencing physical life.* You cannot experience without form, otherwise, you just are.

A time in your evolution is very near where earth will not allow you to remain on it unless you no longer continue to damage it. Earth deserves to exist as do you. Naturally you would want to kill a parasite that is killing your body. So does the earth. Earth has more resources than humans do, just as humans have more resources than parasites. Earth has the ability to reject your existence unless you can learn how to exist on earth without damaging it. Human's energy has changed; it is not in alignment with earth's energy. You are reaching a point where you cannot and will not be able to coexist. Earth can and will annihilate you if needed to survive.

Your souls cannot ever die. Your existence will continue, but on a planet that is more in alignment with your energy. If you all knew how close you were to destroying the human race on earth, you would gladly accept change. You would cease fighting with anyone and anything, including yourselves, and choose only to love and grow spiritually. Doing *"Babaji's Work"* and the *"Heart Technique"* daily would give you the means necessary to evolve rather than devolve on earth.

I will end this book here. It is all up to you. You have a simple, easy way to turn around the pattern of devolving you have been stuck in. Now is the time for evolving with *"Babaji's Work"* and the *"Heart Technique"*. I will help you with anything you need. But, you must be willing to accept My help. This means you must be willing to let go of your mind-made beliefs so you can remember who you truly are.

Questions with Answers from Jesus

The Issue of Being Gay and the Truth about Judging Other People

Some people still believe it is wrong, a "sin", to be gay or to act on it. Will you please give me Your thoughts about this?

Having a natural attraction to the same sex is not wrong, no. The only thing that is wrong is fear-based, separation-resulting judgments, such as this one. Anything that causes you to judge someone as wrong is separating yourself from love, including Me. If someone negatively judges against another for being gay, it is because they themselves fear not being good enough in some way. They feel guilt and shame about something. One cannot judge someone else as wrong without feeling themselves to be wrong in some way. It is a delusional belief system that causes one to judge another as wrong. Yet, if you believe it is wrong, then it is wrong *for you*. You are allowed to perceive however you choose, God grants you that. You have free will always.

The question to ask is how does it make you feel when you judge someone as being wrong? It does not make you feel more loving. It makes you feel more separated from them. Feeling separation always comes from ego, which is not truth. It is an illusion. It is simply a belief. It means nothing. Your beliefs are not who you are. Your beliefs are not who someone else is either. Be willing to see beyond your judgments, please.

Some say that a male's body and a female's body are physically compatible whereas two males or two females are not. That sounds logical. Would you please comment?

You can always find a way to justify judging someone due to the fear you have chosen to believe in; very 'logical' reasons. Believe you are right. Now, ask yourself how you feel about the person(s) you are judging. Do you feel more connected with and loving toward them or do you feel more separate from them? Do not let your so-called logical mind keep you in ignorance of loving each other fully. Pay attention to how you feel. That will always give you a truthful answer. Your mind often does not.

Yet, the Bible and other religions as well state that being gay is a sin. What about that?
There are many discussions in the Bible that I agree with and many that I do not.

What about people who steal, intentionally abuse others or many other forms of hurtful action? I call that wrong and it doesn't seem like an incorrect judgment. Acceptance of such behavior would seem as if I were condoning it. Wouldn't you call that wrong behavior?
To answer your question at the level of the question, yes. When you harm another, it is wrong behavior. A person's behavior of intentionally hurting others is a result of their fear. Instead of judging them for their wrong behavior, which creates separation, love them instead and try to help them heal their pain. Pray for Me to heal them. But, do not judge them.

<u>**The Reason Behind Child Molestation and How to Help**</u>

In truth Jesus, I do not feel love for people with certain horrible behaviors. I feel an aversion toward them. I cannot feel love for a child molester, animal abusers or people that are intentionally harmful to others. And I honestly don't think many other people can love in this way either.
I want to define having judgment toward another. Recognizing a need for healing is not judging someone. When you judge someone, you are making someone "bad" in your perception. You are feeling you are better than they are because you may not do something they do. You are feeling they are less deserving of being loved due to their behavior. You are separating yourself from them in your heart. You

are withholding your love for them. Would you love someone less because they had cancer? It is also a 'sick' perception that causes illness. The perception of a cancer patient manifested a sick body. It is also a sick perception that causes one to intentionally hurt others. How it manifests simply results in a different form of sickness.

Know that a person who consciously abuses others is just as worthy of being given love and compassion, help and healing, as is a person who unconsciously abuses themselves, such as a cancer patient. Both are sick for the exact same reason – a sick perception, resulting from the specific fears in which they believe. Their fears were formed from how they perceived all of their past experiences. Forgive them for not yet being perfect. They are learning how to heal their fear as you also are.

Love them and offer to help them as you would to someone that had cancer. Judge them, look down on them, compare yourself as better than them and you are choosing not to help a child of Mine that is just as worthy of love and compassion as you are. You are unknowingly strengthening feelings that *you* are not worthy of love and compassion, that *you* are sick, that *you* are bad. *Your* perception will become more sick and more fearful. This will cause you more pain and suffering. Your pain and suffering will eventually help you to develop more love and compassion for others and yourself. You will surrender your separating judgmental beliefs eventually when you are willing to let go of them and choose love instead.

In my mind, I get that. Yet in my heart I cannot feel love for everyone. Certainly not for hate-filled people who hurt others intentionally. I cannot seem to forgive it in that I do NOT approve of them or their behavior. I wish I could love more as you do, but in all honesty I do not.
That is okay Connie. You will in time, just be willing. Ask me to help you forgive these types of people and yourself for not loving perfectly yet. That is all that is needed. Just desire to love more. Ask Me to help

you. Ask many times throughout the day. Your willingness can only strengthen if you continue to ask Me.

There are so many child predators, molesters and human traffickers. It is so horrible. What is the reason for this?
Guilt and shame. People that perform these actions have been strongly disapproved of and shunned before they began molesting children. All distorted thinking, emotions and behaviors are a result of not being loved. They are unconsciously seeking love from a child because adults have formed many judgments that children have not yet formed. Child molesters do not feel disapproval with children because children's belief systems have not yet developed disapproving judgment. Child molesters get a distorted version of love through molesting children because they did not and cannot get loving acceptance from adults.

Many psychiatrists and professional therapists believe that such predators are not able to be "cured" and will always continue to molest children if given the opportunity. I believe this is likely true. Therefore, I see only two options for how to deal with them: to kill them or to keep them locked up for the remainder of their lives. No one wants to pay for their existence, including myself. I'm presuming killing them is not what you would recommend. So, what do you recommend doing to help them "heal" and to also protect society from their existence?
Give them this book. Teach them *"Babaji's Work"* and the *"Heart Technique"*. Spiritually evolving is the only way to truly heal any and all malfunctions of the mind. They need to be healed from their past experiences. Killing them will resolve nothing. They are humans and will be reborn on earth again with the same unhealed pain. That is, until the after-earth planet is formed. People with this level of fear are going to be reborn on the after-earth planet.

God will continue bringing you those opportunities which you need to heal and love more until you are able to become willing. The longer you remain unwilling, the more challenging your life will become. Let go of your judgments and love more. If these people were given love, help and healing, this issue would be resolved. Their distorted mind only increases when given more negative judgment which is what caused their behavior in the first place. You need to understand that you are all directly connected. What you give to another, you also give to yourself. You may not see this, but it is true. If you want a healed society, give love. That is what heals anything and everything.

You mentioned that child molesters had fear. They do not seem to be fearful. They are just selfish and uncaring to destroy innocent children's lives and their families. What fear do they have that you are referring to? I'm sorry, but I do not see them as victims. They are victimizers. They know what they are doing and that it is beyond damaging to that child and that it is wrong. But they do it anyway.

They were given various forms of lack of love. Sick people were given sick treatment from others. They fear who they think they are. They fear what they have been taught about who they are. They have deep guilt and shame about who they *believe* they are. All forms of dysfunction are manifested from fear. More disapproval will make them worse. Acknowledge they need to be healed. Help them heal. Give them love and compassion as you would a cancer patient.

I am sorry Jesus, but in truth, I cannot feel love and compassion for those who abuse children and animals.

Give Me your inability to love more by asking Me to help you be willing and capable. Have a genuine desire for the willingness to let go of your judgments that prevent you from loving more like I do. Acknowledge your inability to do this for yourself. Accept that you cannot do this for yourself and ask Me throughout the day to do it for you. If you have an honest and sincere desire to be willing, *I will* enable you. You need to be willing to let go of your strong negative judgment. Continue to believe your judgment is correct and true if you prefer. But, do not stay stuck in that (the judgment). Releasing the judgment is not condoning that behavior. It is simply not fearing it.

Teaching Children about God

Many churches teach stories from the Bible from a perspective which may impart fear, guilt and judgment. So, I would not want my children to learn from these churches. Yet, I want them to understand God and learn how to develop a personal relationship with God. What is a good way for parents to teach their children about God other than going to church? And, what would you recommend to enhance and expand the teachings for those who do receive religious schooling?

If parents taught their children what I am teaching you in this one book alone, they will have a less limited concept of God and know how to develop a personal relationship with God. Teach them to surrender all of their seeming problems to Me - or to "God", if you prefer. If one learns how to surrender, this is all that is needed to live in peace, true happiness and freedom from pain and suffering.

How We Can Create an Enlightened Society

Can you please summarize how we can create an enlightened society?

1. Read My two books transcribed by you and practice what they recommend. Be happy through intentional spiritual growth using the *"Heart Technique"* and healing your suppressed pain by doing *"Babaji's Work"*.
2. Know that when you are willing to surrender your beliefs, this is a surrendering of your ego's identity. Once you do this you would not choose otherwise. But, be reassured by knowing that you can always choose to believe whatever you want. This is your free will. Merely be willing to surrender what may be unknowingly holding you back from feeling more love.

3. Surrender to Me. Give your needs to Me. Surrender the belief that you are ever in control. Only God is in control even when you think you are. Get comfortable with this notion. It will serve you far better going with God than going against God. If you want to control your life or the lives of others, you are going against God. Trust in Me and know that I am God. This is how to achieve the acceptance of "whatever is" and the endless peace that comes with it.
4. Help others heal in any way you can. Seek to improve the lives of others where you can.
5. Bring more balance into your life. You are too busy and have either no time or too little time to relax, still the mind's thoughts and enjoy the present moment.
6. Commune with Me.

The Benefits of Surrendering Control

In our culture today we are taught it is good to "take charge of your life" and we should all feel in control of our lives, especially women. Isn't it at all a good thing to have control over our own lives? Why is it beneficial to feel we do not have control?

Because you do not. The sooner you acknowledge this, the sooner you are able to have peace. Then inner joy develops. Then more love, then compassion, then forgiveness and then gratitude. Then comes the desire to give that to others and you continue to cultivate more and more of each. "Walk with Me" means you give Me your life. Giving Me your life means you ask Me for what you need – everything, every day. Then, you begin to access My power in your life. You begin to receive miracles upon miracles.

Surrender is the absolute most powerful way to attain the peace of God regardless of your circumstances. Know that when you are able to surrender (accept) your unwanted circumstances, the need to undergo unwanted experiences will vanish. Enlightenment is inevitable when you become adept at surrender.

I do not fully understand how to "accept whatever is". That sounds like we walk around totally numb, not having any emotions and not caring too much about anything. This doesn't sound very appealing to me. Can you please explain this further?

You are able to care without fear. This is the difference. The amount of caring is maximized to your highest potential when you are without fear. The presence of fear diminishes your ability to care and experience love and peace and bliss. Without fear, you would experience fullness of life and ecstatic joy. Surrender is the best tool and the only way to be free of all fear. You do not become less of who you are. You become more of who you are (love).

<u>Soul Desires Versus Ego Desires</u>

Is it better to give up our desires? Is it better not to have desires? Would it be better to automatically trust that whatever is happening comes from God and therefore "should be" happening? And, that we show our trust in God by simply "knowing" that You bring us all we should have…and, without our having to ask?

No Connie. Do not give up your desires. Have desires, have desires, have desires. You are here on earth to experience your personal desires. Enjoy them. If a desire is not yet manifesting, accept that situation with ease and grace. You do this by trusting in Me.

If a desire of yours has not yet been fulfilled, it is because it will not bring you what you think it will. It will not be for your highest good. You may not always believe this, but it is always true.

That being said, I would like to explain the difference between a soul desire and an ego desire. If you feel worry, fear, need, frustration or any level of attachment to your desire, it is not a desire detached from its outcome. It is an ego wanting something more to fill the continuous lack it feels; the lack of feeling fulfilled. A soul desire is what you want when you already feel full. And guess what your soul's desire(s) will be? It will not be for anything more. It will be the desire to give [expand] more of your fullness to others.

Giving your fullness is the only natural soul desire you could ever have when you feel fullness within. When you do not know what fullness means, your desires are tainted with fear. And, it is this ego fear that knows only of what comes through the physical reality. Therefore, it wants something that is a manifestation in the physical existence. And, if that desire is achieved, the satisfaction never lasts. You will want more and more or become fearful of losing it.

All desires are natural and it is okay to have them. It is okay to 'want'. And always, you can go to God for anything. It is never wrong to ask God – for anything.

But, also know there is another level of desire. In time, you will come to the place where you will be given everything you desire, and more, without even needing to ask. When you can go directly to the Creator, you need not ask about the details of that which has already been created for you.

Desire first your conscious contact with the presence of God. For when you are connected directly to the Supplier, you need not concern yourself about the supply. Complete in the state of acceptance, your needs and desires are supplied before you even know of them. So, connect with God, the Supplier of all, first. Then everything else is easy.

One of my friends thinks it would make her a lot happier if she and her husband had a nice boat to enjoy. They aren't able to afford one yet. Would You please comment?
If she is able to be happy without the boat, this will be the most helpful thing she can do to gain the support she needs to get a boat. Surrender your desire to Me. Ask Me to manifest your desire for you. If it is My will, it will happen. If it is My will, it is because it will be

beneficial for you to have it. Trust and know this so you can accept whatever the outcome. It is your *need* (attachment) for a desire that prevents you from attracting it. Because you feel you *need* it, there is fear of not getting it. This also establishes the firm belief in your mind that you do *not* have it – you *need* it and that it is lacking from your life. This fear blocks you from being able to receive it. Want it, desire it, but do not think you need it to be happy or content.

A friend of mine works a dead end, low wage job that she dislikes. She has to work too many hours just to survive. She wants a more enjoyable, less stressful job that pays more so she can have a more balanced life; a healthier, happier and more peaceful life. But, she is not getting another job. Can you please comment?

This friend of yours will not accept a better job. She knows what she would really like to do, what she naturally enjoys and is very talented at. She has not attempted to get a job doing what she would really like to do because she does not feel good enough to receive a better job. It is only her mind's beliefs from her mind-made reality that convinces her she is not capable of getting a better job. She has the unconscious beliefs that she has to work hard and do what she does not enjoy, sacrifice her sleep, happiness and health, work many hours and struggle to survive in this world. She adopted her father's beliefs about this. This is why she has not been given a better job. If you do not receive your desires, ask Me to bring what you need to enable you to receive it. Be open to accept a new way of thinking. Be open to new knowledge that comes your way. If you are struggling through life just to survive, you need to change your thinking. You need to make progress evolving spiritually to increase your awareness of what is holding you back from achieving a better quality life. Having the right education, the right connections, the right professional experience, the 'right' physical appearance, age, race or sex, are unnecessary. They can be advantageous, but they are all unnecessary. All you need is Me. Come to Me. I can bring you your heart's desires more effectively if you can learn to allow God to be in charge of your life. This book tells you everything you need to know to learn how to do that.

Surrender – It's All You Really Need

I think you are saying: "I, God, am more powerful than any imagined limitation in anyone's life and all that anyone needs is to come to "ME". It is God who is really in charge anyway (believe it or not) and God is willing and able to bring all that is needed to accomplish anyone's heart's desire. Miracles come from consciously putting God in charge".

I am comparing what you just said to what I remember reading from countless self-help books. There are many books, programs and methods which inspire, motivate and try to teach individuals to access their subconscious powers, proper methods for using the law of attraction, visualization and affirmations to increase abundance and prosperity, and so-called "secrets" that successful people apply to get all they want out of life. Yet for the millions of these books read or seminars attended, I don't think there are millions of successful outcomes. If it worked, this would be a country of only happy people, probably all millionaires. Can you please comment?

Yes. I agree. These "self-help" ways can be helpful, yet to a limited degree. The power to create unlimited miracles comes from God. You are able to attract or create unlimited miracles by intentionally giving (surrendering) your desires to God. He will manifest them for you. Surrendering to God is a more fulfilling, productive and easier way to receive your desires. If you master the art of surrender, the rest is easy.

How would you direct an atheist to surrender to God? You are teaching us to go beyond our beliefs. Yet, if one does not believe in God, how can one surrender to God?

They are going to have challenges in surrendering effectively until they do. It is as simple as that. It is not for Me to sway their beliefs if they are not wanting to. If one can acknowledge there is a creative intelligence which is a higher power than oneself alone, they can surrender to this.

But is that just as good?
A "higher power" that is not derived from love is a very limited higher power. But in time, it will grow into more.

What exactly do you mean by a "higher power"?
A creative, coordinating intelligence - which is a power greater than you alone.

<u>Words to Describe God</u>

Some people become guarded when they hear the name "Jesus", but not when they hear "Christ Consciousness" or the name "God". Some are fine with using words such as: "Creator" or "Higher Power", but not "God". Others may prefer words like:

Invisible Power	Life Energy
Love Energy	Higher Self
Force	Source
Soul	Spirit
Holy Spirit	Field of Unlimited Possibilities
Quantum Field	The Divine
Divine Mind	Divine Presence
Divine Wisdom	Pure Consciousness
Pure Awareness	Coordinator of the Universe
Universal Intelligence	Supreme Being
Lord	The Absolute

Does it matter which words one uses in referring to Jesus or God? Do You have a personal preference?
No and no. They are only words. Some people do pay more attention to language than to what is behind the words. Call the Creator whatever you choose. It does not make any difference to Me what words you choose; no.

Do you, Jesus, prefer that people believe You are God?
No. What you think or believe has no meaning to Me. What you *feel*, though, has extreme meaning to Me. Please just love.

Without Beliefs, Who Are You?

I know some Christians who become upset when confronted with people who do not believe in your divinity the same way as they do. I have one friend who feels it is her righteous duty to stand up and defend you Jesus, as our only Lord and Savior. In her devotion to you she sometimes alienates others – all due to the differences in their beliefs. What would you tell my friend?
She is feeling threatened because she believes her beliefs are who she is. A belief that is different from hers seems to threaten the existence of who she thinks she is. Your ego does not want to become less than what it is and if someone takes away just one single belief it has formed, it will be less than what it was. Ego wants to strengthen, not decrease. A stronger belief creates a stronger resistance (fear). Your mind-made self always feels insecure because it can never be real. It is easily threatened. Ego is only a temporary and illusory reality that is formed from the accumulation of many beliefs. Take away all your beliefs and you are not "you" anymore. This is scary for the ego. For then the real you becomes your new reality.

> *The real you does not care about beliefs.*
> *The real you is beyond beliefs.*

No one's beliefs can threaten Me. When you develop more awareness that you are as much a part of other people as of yourself, this feeling will dissolve away. Remember, it is not your beliefs that you want to hang onto. You want to let them go so you can realize the true you.

> *The true you is found behind your beliefs.*

You will become less threatened by the differences stemming from the beliefs of others when you remember who you really are – one with all. Each and every one of the "all" had different experiences formed by their unique perception, resulting in differing beliefs. When you understand this, you will honor, love, cherish and adore their differences as I do.

Notice that when you seek others of like mind, such as religious or social groups, there is also the subtlety of seeking those of similar beliefs. This is done to strengthen your own beliefs, calming the fearful ego. The ego believes that the more who agree with you, the truer and more powerful your own beliefs become. This strengthens the ego's identity. Likewise, the ego's power is threatened by differing beliefs. You all want your own version of reality to be supported by others.

But, who would I be if I had no more beliefs? If I had no more beliefs, I would not be anybody. Wouldn't I be more like a vegetable that cannot think or feel? The concept is confusing.
You would still be who you are but without what the mind-made self believes you are. I do not have beliefs. I do not believe. I know.

You are not what you think. I am not what I think. I am the pure "presence" that is behind the thinking-self. When you are living in your human body, but also have become fully aware, you can still use your mind to think. But you will also have the realization that you are not your thoughts; you are not your beliefs.

> *Fully aware, you realize that who you are is*
> *Beyond your thoughts or beliefs.*

More intellectual understanding comes with increased awareness of your true-self. As you progress in your awareness, *"Being"* begins to predominate. This is beyond what your mind can fully understand.

I will give you some simple sentences to help you understand the nature of the mind-made self and the true self:

- The mind thinks and believes that what it thinks is real.
- The mind-made self (ego-identity) believes that it *is* what the mind thinks and believes.
- True-self *knows*. It *knows* it is not the mind's thoughts and beliefs. True-self's awareness goes beyond thoughts and beliefs.
- When you are enlightened, yet still in a human body, you will still think, but you will know you are not your thoughts.
- The 'real' you, the eternal you who never dies, is the witness behind the ego's perception.
- The ego's beliefs are formed and reinforced through the perception of your experiences. Judgments accumulate in your mind and over time become associated as your only identity. I enjoy this and not that, I am this kind of person and not that sort, this is good and that is bad, that is right and this is wrong. All of these *beliefs* become your only known identity. You identify with these beliefs as being who you are; as being the truth of who you are.

Jesus Interprets from the Bible

"For God so loved the world that He gave His only begotten Son that who so ever believeth in Him should not perish, but have everlasting life." John 3:16

I've been told by Christians that Jesus died for our sins; that Jesus died on the cross so that we could all be "saved". This means that as believers, we all go to Heaven after we die. Non-believers don't make it there. All this implies that we must believe in You. So, if our beliefs are actually irrelevant, what is the true meaning about this core Christian belief?

"Believe in Me" means believe in My teachings. Come to *know* My teachings are truth. Everything I teach is to help you *know* that you are God as much as I am. Everything I teach is to help you realize who you are - the real, eternal you that has been hidden behind your beliefs.

When words are used to describe God there will always be limitations to understanding, such as these. There will be room for error with interpreting them according to each person's level of awareness. Know that the Kingdom of Heaven is within you already. Heaven is not a tangible location that you go to after the death of your body. Having full awareness of God *is* being in the Kingdom of Heaven. Please know it is possible to experience this while still living in your physical body.

All fear must be realized, honored and accepted to become free of it. You will fully realize you are God again only in the absence of fear. All fear comes from believing you are separate from God, separate from love. You cannot know God through your beliefs.

A belief about God is only what you think about God. Knowing God comes from experiencing God.

You experience God through the heart, not through the mind's beliefs. The heart *feels*. It does not believe. Feeling more love for yourself and others until you have weeded out all fear is the only way to come to know God. I will give you a simple example that demonstrates how you cannot fully understand God through the mind's beliefs alone.

If you have never tasted an apple, I could explain to you in great detail just what an apple tastes like. I could tell you it is sweet and a little tart; that it not as soft as a peach and is crispy, but not as strongly scented and with a slightly different taste. You can imagine and fully "believe" everything I tell you about how an apple tastes. But, you will never *know* what an apple really tastes like without having the direct experience.

Can you see how "knowing" from the mind alone is a very limited level of understanding? Believing in God through the mind is not experiencing God. I want you to go beyond your mere beliefs about God. I want you to experience God. Only then will you truly *know* God. You will then have the awareness that we are all one and not separate. All of you are capable of knowing God directly if you are willing to go beyond your beliefs.

"Verily, verily, I say unto you, he that believeth on Me, the works that I do shall he also do; and greater works than these shall he do; because I go unto My Father. John 14:12

What is the meaning of this verse?
It means that you also will be able to create great miracles as you become enlightened. That is, when you come to realize that God is within you; that you are God and that you have all the unlimited power of God within you. Then, you will be able to do what I did and even more. You will be as unlimited in your ability to create miracles as I am, when you also know the truth of who you are – God.

What does "because I go unto My Father" mean?
It means because I give Myself to my Father. I surrender Myself to My Father. It means to give My desire to My Higher Power, the power of God.

And what exactly do You mean by "surrender myself to my Father"? Surrender what?
Your life; your will; your need; your desire; whatever you are resisting.

How do we surrender our life to God? I'm not sure I fully understand how to do that.
You live your life in the way I did. You choose to love yourself and others. You choose to have patience, compassion and care for others. You live your life for God. You do this by living to love and care for others. You live to help make others happy, whole and useful. You help heal

the wounded. You feed the hungry. You house the homeless. You help prevent abuse and mistreatment to all beings on earth. You seek God's grace. You intentionally evolve spiritually and help others do the same.

What exactly do you mean when you say, "seek God's grace"?
Seek the gift of reunion with all.

Why won't God, or You give me this now if I am asking for it? If I am Your child, shouldn't I be entitled to this simply by genuinely asking for it? I am asking for You after all, our Father. Why can't I be graced with that now? Why does it have to be such a slow arduous route? Why do I have to be denied this even for one day? That just doesn't seem right to me.
You are not able to accept God's grace until you love yourself enough to give yourself to Him. Our Father is waiting for you. You are not waiting for Him.

How do I love myself enough to give myself to Him?
You live your life in the way I did, as I just described. This cultivates more and more self-love. You can only develop more self-love by *giving* love – *expressing* your love – *experiencing* more love with others. And in time, you will receive God's grace - the full awareness of the full experience of God – union with all. This is My level of awareness or what some also call "unity consciousness" or "Christ consciousness".

It is hard for me to imagine living in our physical world with this level of awareness. Can you please describe what our life in this world would be like when we are in unity consciousness?
Yes. You do what you love to do each moment. Your direct experience in life is filled with absolute love, joy and peace. There is not an ounce of fear. There is no such thing as dysfunction or lack. Negative judgment does not exist; nor does feeling separate with anything or anyone. You live your life with ecstatic joy and have so much gratitude toward our Father for your life. You gain so much pleasure and fulfillment by

helping others achieve this state of awareness. Your heart is so full of love there is no more room for pain. The mind will not be able to fully understand this experience. It is an experience, not a belief.

Was Your Death Really Our Salvation?

No. Your sins were already forgiven before I was born as Jesus Christ. I saved you before I was born as Jesus Christ. You all had the free will to accept Me or crucify Me as you did. Whether you chose to accept or reject Me, you were already forgiven and saved. My being born as Jesus was to help you know you were already forgiven. My life was to help create a more loving consciousness on earth. My existence, My life on earth as Jesus Christ is what saved you, not My death.

Jesus Defines Sin

What is your definition of the word sin?
Any thought, belief, feeling or action that does not come from God (love). Any thought, belief, feeling or action that comes from fear. All fears manifest judgments (beliefs) that cause negative emotions such as, anger, resentment, hate, blame, guilt, shame, self-pity, loneliness, sorrow, jealousy, worry, insecurity, envy, lust, which means any imbalanced desire. All of these fear-based emotions are "sins". These emotions originally occur from the incorrect belief that you are separate from God.

Recommended Reading From Jesus

Are there any particular books you recommend reading?
Yes. Whatever books make you feel able to love more.

I Want a Daily Spiritual Practice – So Why Don't I Do it?

Sometimes I find it challenging to do *"Babaji's Work"* and the *"Heart Technique"* daily. It doesn't take much time, but frankly,

at times I just do not feel like doing it. It is like I am resisting it at some level. Would you please comment?
You do not feel like doing it because your ego does not want to die. The ego perceives any movement toward the peace of God with resistance. Know that ego will find all sorts of 'logical' reasons why you cannot do it today. When you become tired enough of feeling unfulfilled and weary enough from a less than joyous life, you will disregard your reasons for avoiding intentional spiritual growth and will choose to heal your heart and expand your soul. You will just do it.

When you eventually realize that nothing in the physical world can give you the feeling of completeness, peace or inner joy, you will then become willing to intentionally develop spiritually. You achieve fullness of life by becoming more aware of God – of your soul. After you develop the habit of doing *"Babaji's Work"* and the *"Heart Technique"* daily, it will not be a challenge. You will begin to feel the benefits from doing it and this will naturally become a priority in your life.

The benefits you will start noticing are: increased peace, inner joy with a sense of wonder for life; lack of fear and worry; more love, compassion, forgiveness and gratitude develop. Drama fades away. You will naturally increase your awareness of the present moment. Healing occurs on all levels and the benefits of this are too many to list in words. God begins to predominate in your life. Miracles are a daily occurrence. Your desires are spontaneously fulfilled without effort. Limitations become obsolete.

Why Jesus Was Born into the Jewish Faith

Why were you born into the Jewish faith? Is there any particular reason?
Yes. The people of Jewish faith had more guilt than all other faiths put together. I wanted to give them an opportunity to heal it. My

being born as a Jew could have helped them heal their guilt fully if they had accepted me.

Why did they have more guilt than all other people?
They were a collection of people that had extreme guilt due to how they chose to perceive (judge) their past experiences from prior lifetimes. People with similar egoic beliefs are often born into a group of people (culture) with similar forms of pain and fear. "Like attracts like" is a natural law in creation.

Why did they have so much guilt from their prior lifetimes?
They began judging others harshly as a result of the fear of separation from God that they felt. They felt insecure and not good enough. They chose to ignore their fear through developing a superiority complex in their prior lifetimes. They gave others extreme judgment, criticism and rejection to help them mask their own fears of feeling incomplete; their fear of not being good enough. They were stuck in their separating judgment for a long time and they accumulated more fear. As always, what you give out will eventually come back to you. They needed to bring balance to the energy they gave others in prior lifetimes. God will always bring you what you need to heal your fears.

How does someone effectively heal guilt or any other forms of pain and fear?
Ask Me to heal it for you. Surrender it to Me. Do *"Babaji's Work"* and the *"Heart Technique"* daily.

Why the Holocaust Happened

Why is it that the Jewish faith experienced the Holocaust?
It is the same answer. They had such deep guilt and shame they unconsciously created (attracted) a strong experience of rejection and mistreatment. Doing *"Babaji's Work"* and the *"Heart Technique"* daily will prevent *all* of you from attracting painful experiences that enable

you to face and heal your pain and fear. Remember to surrender your pain and fear to Me. Ask Me to heal it as you are honoring it.

Have they healed much of their guilt?
No. They are hanging onto it for dear life. All of you are hanging onto your fears in the form of judgments for dear life; the ego's life. Until you have the willingness to go beyond ego – your beliefs, your judgments, your fears, you will attract more painful experiences. Save yourselves this unnecessary and arduous route to achieve enlightenment. Become willing to face your fears and awaken your soul. This means do *"Babaji's Work"* and the *"Heart Technique"*.

<u>Destiny and Free Will</u>

Will you explain the difference between destiny and free will?
Destiny and free will are taking place simultaneously. Before you were born, your soul chose certain events to occur during your lifetime. These self-chosen conditions are your destiny. That which your soul continues to choose as you progress throughout your lifetime may also be called your destiny. Your free will is your self-chosen response to those self-chosen experiences.

Your soul chooses your destiny with the purpose of helping you learn how to experience and express more of the love that you already are; to become more of who you truly are. If you use your free will to respond to life with love, compassion and non-judgment to yourself and to others, your soul will choose certain "destined" experiences to help you continue to love more. If your free will is used to respond with fear, your soul will create different "destined" experiences to help you learn what is needed to be capable of loving more. The ongoing destined experiences your soul chooses for you changes depending on how you choose to respond to such experiences. Destiny always gives the opportunity to overcome more fear and experience a higher level of loving.

So, our soul chooses and creates our experiences? Isn't it God that creates and chooses our experiences?
Yes. It is one and the same. This question shows you perceive God as being a separate entity. Remember that God is not an individual person, physical being or even a spiritual being who is separate from you. God, our Father, is pure love energy which comprises every single atom of the universe, including you.

But I am a female human being with the name of Connie Fox, right?
Yes. You are also the formless life energy within Connie Fox's physical body. This is the true you who never dies. This is your spirit-self; your soul. This is our Father made manifest.

You <u>are</u> God expressing.

All of you are learning to become more aware of the love that you already are. This love energy *is* your soul, your 'higher' self, your "God-self". This *is* God. When enlightened, you experience your physical identity while at the same time knowing who you are *beyond* your physical identity. You will all reach this state of awareness and create Heaven on earth for everyone.

The Belief that Spirit Communication is Evil

One of my religious friends says the Bible states that anyone who communicates with spirit – the spirit of Jesus, angels or the deceased is doing "evil work" and that it is really Satan or Satan's helpers with whom they are communicating. This kind of bothers me. What do you say to this?
There are words added, withheld, altered and misinterpreted in the Bible. It is okay Connie that some believe your communication gift is the "work of Satan" or that they should fear you. Remember that everyone's beliefs will vary depending on the experiences they have had and how they have chosen to judge them. You are feeling

threatened because you do not know who you are. If you did, you would know and understand these others have chosen to believe in something they have learned and you would not take it personally. Someone else's beliefs would not threaten you. You would also choose not to judge them in response to them judging you.

That is all Connie. Love everyone, regardless of their beliefs. Their fearful and separating beliefs are an illusion, as your fearful and separating beliefs are also. What you believe to be truth is your version of reality. Both of you are 'right' in your reality. Remember your beliefs are not who you are. Be willing to see who others are beyond their beliefs – and beyond your own beliefs also. Do not stay stuck in judging her judgment of you.

I do know and understand that she simply believes in what she has been taught. But, it still irritates me. Would you please comment? It is okay to feel irritated Connie. Do not resist feeling irritated. Do *"Babaji's Work"* with this negative emotion. Do not think about your friend or others that may have the same belief or about how wrong you think her beliefs are. Just intentionally feel this feeling – irritation. With this irritation, you also feel frustrated, offended, hurt, disapproved of, rejected, unappreciated, not good enough and unloved. You feel these feelings not because of her, but because you feel separate from God, separate from love, wholeness, fullness. You have forgotten who you are - one with all – united with God, Me and everyone as 'one'. Each individual of the 'one' has different unique perceptions, formed from their beliefs based on varying experiences. Give yourself a little time to feel this as fully as you can, until the intensity of it subsides. Do *"Babaji's Work"* on it until it does not bother you anymore. It will not take long. You just need to honor your egoic fear-based feelings to grow beyond them.

This friend also believes, as do some others, that the end of the Biblical times, 2,000 years ago, was the end of all legitimate prophecy. She believes there used to be "real" and "good" spirit

and angel communicators before, called prophets. But, there have not been anymore since then. Further, any communications with spirit or Jesus or God is false – or even sinful. She even fears it as leading to demonic influence and the path of Satan. How does it not bother you that people have such mistaken beliefs?

Would you love your eight year old child more than your four year old child, simply because your eight year old child may understand more? No, you would not. This is how I see all of My children.

Believing in Satan

My friend says that Satan can disguise himself as Jesus or one of Your loving angels and "trick" us into believing they are good or that "following" them is doing something good, when in actuality they are not from You, but from Satan; as a "wolf in sheep's clothing". How can one really tell if something is 'good' and comes from God and not from the evil force of Satan?

Learn how to feel from your heart, not your mind. Fear does not come from the heart. All fear is an illusion, which comes from ego – a fear-based perception. The mind's perception *can* be very tricky. A helpful general guideline to determine if something could lead you away from God is to notice if it makes you feel more fearful. Remember that Satan can do nothing to you unless you empower him with your belief in him. When you believe in Satan, you are putting your faith in Satan rather than Me. Do you really believe that Satan is more powerful than Me? If so, you are supporting and strengthening Satan's influence in your life rather than God's influence. I am more powerful than Satan. Think of Me and My love. There is nothing more powerful than My love. If you truly trusted in Me, you would not fear Satan and he would have no power over you. Grow beyond the limited belief that Satan can harm you. With trust in me you are invisible to Satan.

The Nature of an Animal's Soul

Do animals have a soul? What happens to them when they die? When we die, are we reunited with our beloved pets? And if so, is it just an illusion since their bodies do not actually exist anymore? Yes, their souls are the same as humans. Instead of being positioned in a human body, they are positioned in an animal body. They are not lower-evolved beings as some of you think. Some animals are more highly aware than humans. Animals chose to come here on earth for one purpose only; not for them but for you. They are here to help you learn how to love unconditionally. They do this simply by example.

When you see their bodies after death, it is an illusion, yes. But, it is also real. You may see them in their bodily form as they were before. Technically this is an illusion since their body is no longer. In most cases, you reunite with Me, our Father and the souls of your loved ones including your beloved pets. Then, your consciousness expands and becomes unlimited again and the temporary illusionary forms become realized as all "one"; no longer in any one specific limited form. This is Heaven. Remember it is possible to have this unlimited awareness while living in your physical body. This is the ultimate goal; becoming God-realized; finding the Kingdom of God within you.

After We Die, Do We Remain in Heaven For Eternity?

Eternal heaven comes when you have attained God-realization while in your physical body. You are intended to experience life being God-realized.

Is There Only One True Path to God?

Most religions believe that their specific teachings are the only true path to God. They can't all be right, can they? Would you please comment?

All of you will eventually learn how to love as fully as I do. This is your only goal – to learn how to love fully as I do. What you believe about Me or God truly means nothing. Your ability to love more as I do has nothing to do with holding the beliefs of a Christian or a Buddhist or a Hindu or an Atheist. Such religions are belief systems. You will never know God from having a specific belief system. If being a Christian helps you feel more loving, then being a Christian is "right" for you. If being a Hindu makes you feel more loving, then being a Hindu is right for you. If having no religious belief system makes you feel able to love more, then having no religion is just what you need at this time.

You are each at different levels in your ability to love fully. What is needed to help you learn to love more will continue to change throughout time. If it doesn't change, you are not growing spiritually. Be careful about believing that others should be on the same path you are on. Everyone's spiritual journey toward God comes in differing forms and may also change throughout one's lifetime. Your present path may be right for now, but that does not mean it is right for someone else at this time.

Do not think you know better than God what is best for another.

God unfolds everyone's life just perfectly.

"Babaji's Work" is a technique that teaches how to effectively heal all suppressed, unhealed emotional pain from past experiences, which dissolves away underlying fears that are the real cause of your pain.

Following are the summaries of *"Babaji's Work"* **from my first book,** *"The Power of You"*:

Extended Summary of Babaji's Work

From Mahavatar Babaji:
Be alone, be comfortable. Think of what you are mostly distressed about right now. What is bothering you the most right now? Put your attention on one issue at a time. Start with the most bothersome issue.

Now that you have the most bothersome issue acknowledged, how is it making you feel? Think about your feelings now; not the issue, not about how valid you are for feeling the way you do. Do not think you are bad, wrong or weak for feeling the way you do. Do not judge yourself. Do not judge the person or situation that has you feeling as you are. What are you feeling most now from this issue? Identify the emotion. Name it.

Do you feel fearful, worried, inadequate, anger, resentment, jealousy, sorrow, regret, resentment, frustration, shame, guilt, helpless, hopeless, unloved, unwanted, uncared about, ugly, undesirable, lonely, empty, lost, confused, afraid, nervous, insecure, cowardly, abused, victimized, abandoned, betrayed, humiliated, devastated, hateful toward someone, toward God, toward Jesus, toward me, toward yourself, unappreciated, not good enough, unworthy, completely worthless, stupid, pathetic, sick, overwhelmed, insane?

Identify which feeling is the strongest. Listen to a song that repeats my mantra or repeat it yourself, silently or out loud for about ten minutes. Now honor this feeling by giving it your sole attention. Sit or lay there undistracted and try to feel this particular feeling. Do not think about why you feel this feeling. You are already justified for having this feeling. You are genuinely validated for feeling this feeling. Now feel it – intently. Feel how deep this pain is. Ignore nothing. Just feel it.

If you are having trouble feeling it more deeply or trouble feeling anything, think back to a memory of when you felt this same or similar feeling. Think of some experience that made you feel bad in a similar way – hurt, fearful, angry, etc. Think back to that time, to that experience. Feel what you felt then. Feel it intently, as deeply as you can. Stay with that feeling until it subsides naturally; until it lessens and lightens and you now feel ready to let it go and get back to your day.

Do this every day at least once. Do it more often as you would like. You cannot overdo this, but keep each session under an hour. Some may naturally feel finished within a few minutes, sometimes longer. Some days you will be able to experience the feeling more deeply, other times, less so. Accept whatever comes. Allow whatever comes and know it will pass. Know it is only a feeling. The feeling itself cannot hurt you. The feeling will not kill you. But the resisting of it can. When you do this, you are not resisting it; you are facing and honoring it. This is what will free you from all your pain, all your judgments, all your fears. This will bring you to God's feet - the place you need to reach to surrender to our Beloved Christ - to surrender to God with total love, compassion and non-judgment.

Do not be afraid to feel – ever. Negative feelings are merely feelings. They are illusions, but very real to you now. You will come to know they are illusions only by facing and feeling them – giving them your attention – honoring them. Their power over you will quickly diminish. Soon, you will be able to laugh at them when they arise. You will know they are not you. You will know they are not real. They are harmless, meaningless and insignificant. Then your power of God, of love, will begin to expand in ways you cannot imagine.

When you begin again, start with the beginning of this summary. Doing this every day will free you quickly. Listen to my mantra in a song or repeat it silently in your mind or out loud for ten minutes or more before beginning.

Then pour your heart out to Christ and our Father. This means feel your love and devotion to Them. Simply honor Them and ask Them for union.

Additional note: The exact pronunciation of my mantra, *"Om Namah Shivaya"* is not important. But, Connie will display the typical pronunciation of my mantra. Remember its meaning:

"I surrender to you God" or "Lord, Thy will be done" or "I bow/surrender to my higher inner self". It is intentionally asking God (love) to awaken you – to expand within. Repetition of my mantra releases your pain and fears more effectively than anything else ever has or ever will.

Om Na-mah Shee-vi-ya

Brief Summary of Babaji's Work

1. Be Alone. Be comfortable.
2. Think about what is disturbing you the most today or at this time.
3. Define what the feeling is; do not think about it.
4. Know you are justified and validated for feeling this.
5. Listen to my mantra or repeat it silently or out loud for about ten minutes or as long as you like.
6. Intentionally feel this feeling as deeply as you can. Do not judge it, just feel it.
7. When the feeling subsides naturally, get back to your day.
8. If you have trouble feeling deeply or identifying any feeling, remember a past experience that caused you to feel a similar way. Or, think of any memory that caused you pain. Then remember the feeling of this pain and feel it as deeply as you can.
9. Do at least one session every day. Feel each and every pain in your heart. Do this with every painful memory you have. Do this until they are gone.
10. Then you will be at the one pain you have left to heal – the pain from the perceived loss of God. Feel this pain and you will then be set free. Ask God for union – for wholeness with yourself, for wholeness with all.

You can heal the pain in your heart this way or by going through numerous "real" painful events in your life. Until you acknowledge, face and feel them all, they remain with you. Honor them now (in your mind and in your heart) without needing the actual experiences to accomplish this. This is the quicker, easier path to Christ consciousness.

You will heal them quickly if you are willing. If unwilling, you will heal them slowly.

Om Na-mah Shee-vi-ya

What Mette has to say about the "Heart Technique"

The goal of my life has always been enlightenment. Long ago I had conjured up an idea of how to gain a higher level of awareness. I prayed to reach my soul's full potential – that elusive utopia of permanent peace and bliss. So, I embraced years of deep meditation visiting retreats and ashrams all over the world. I pursued mind expanding workshops, seminars and teaching courses, as well as a professional career development in Denmark as a licensed Teacher, Counselor and Psychomotor Physical Therapist. Yet, nothing in my life had been quite as spectacular as when Connie channeled the Heart Technique to me from Jesus.

The divine timing of the universe kept me in suspense for half of a year. I had chosen to retire from teaching, trusting that my best new path was soon to appear. Because I allowed myself time to visit with Connie in Florida, the new course in my life was revealed to me. After a meditation, I joined Connie out on our porch to share the beautiful mood of a tropical morning. That very morning, Jesus gave me the Heart Technique through Connie.

Jesus told me I had already gained both the intellectual and experiential knowledge to understand what disconnects people from their soul's peace, love and stillness. I had grown quite adept at recognizing the difference between love and fear and the endless forms in which it manifests into one's belief system. Looking back, I now see how I had been prepared. Now, I was ready to bring the Heart Technique to the world.

The Heart Technique is a daily practice that combines five advanced techniques, designed to increase the inner awareness of one's soul. As it says on the cover of this book,

> *"There is a big difference between*
> *<u>Believing you have</u> an eternal soul*
> *And the direct experience of <u>knowing</u>*
> *<u>You are</u> an eternal soul."*

The Heart Technique is designed to bring that experience into your life and give yourself all the love and compassion you've been seeking and longing for.

These five techniques work together in synchronicity. Each step builds itself forward in a distinctive and unified way. The program is one daily session of thirty-five minutes, with each step being performed back-to-back simultaneously. Although there are some practices which may appear similar, the combination of these particular five steps used together and experienced in this order of sequence, makes it such a unique and effective tool for spiritual growth. The Heart Technique comes from ancient knowledge, yet implemented in a new way.

A few quotes from people who have learned the Heart Technique™:

- *"After having been introduced to The Heart Technique I have practiced it every day with joy and enthusiasm. I feel an inner peace I have not felt before. It is easier for me to handle the chaos in my outer world because my inner world is now at peace. I am much better at handling stress, anger and irritation when it comes. I have obtained more happiness in my everyday life. It is fantastic".*

  Pernille P. - Falster, Denmark

- *"The Heart Technique has given me a deeper meaning of my life. I have without a doubt, gained more peace in my mind and I feel more and more okay being who I am. I have become more openhearted towards myself as well as others. My spirit feels more alive and I experience more guidance and support in my daily life. I am very grateful".*

Catherine M. - Copenhagen, Denmark

- *"I felt a peace, a freedom from unease and tension; like a blanket of love, peace and comfort covered me wholly within my being. It felt delightful and so right. My mind automatically thought, "ahhhhh...this is what I have been yearning for. This is who I really am. I need absolutely nothing".*

Susan F. – Palm Beach Gardens, FL USA

- *"Through The Heart Technique I have been reminded about how important it is to feel and experience and not only to know things in our head. Throughout life I have become much better at loving myself, but through the Heart technique I have experienced the core feeling of loving myself. That was a huge experience and I am very grateful".*

Bent B. - Falster, Denmark

- *"Mette reaches ones soul as well as one's mind. She makes it easy and simple to learn The Heart Technique. I have grown into a much more clear version of who I am and I have gained much more peace and trust in life, in the universe and in the fact that everything is good. My pain from a lifetime of coping with Multiple Sclerosis has been cut in more than half. I still notice it, but it is not a part of my life anymore and I have only been doing it several weeks now. I have gained more energy, joy and peace in a wonderful and intriguing way".*

Susanne. A. - Falster, Denmark

- *"I feel a wise being has entered my body".*

Rosemary L. – Bristol, England

- *"This is so big".*

Helene G. - Odense, Denmark

In Closing from the Author

After the editing of this book, Jesus gave me special instruction ***not*** to communicate with Him so regularly for now. Instead, I was now to speak directly to God the Father. Although I had conversed with God many times before, I was quite challenged by this new situation for at some level, I felt somewhat abandoned; even fearful to "let go" of Jesus. I had come to rely upon Jesus to guide Me throughout my daily life and had developed a close personal connection with Him.

The feeling of his presence during our talks is very distinctive to me. I have a picture of Him in my mind and I feel His presence as both human and divine. Still, Jesus specifically directed me to literally by-pass Him and speak my thoughts and desires and any questions directly to our Father.

Sharing words with God is certainly exceptional and loving. Yet in my mind, I could not quite "picture" God. He is the formless, un-manifest energy, who is the First Source and Creator of all there is. Yet, I admit I did not feel the total love, devotion and trust in my heart as I did with Jesus. In truth, I did not "know" the reality of God in my heart. Jesus pointed out to me that He is also our Father, but in a manifest form. Also, that my relationship with Jesus had developed over time and that my relationship with God would also grow in time.

Finally, I asked God to fix this situation for me and to help me get to know Him better. God told me the following in conversation and from it, I began to feel more personally and lovingly connected with our divine Father. Later, I understood why Jesus directed me in this way. He told me to remember how God is within me. I had somehow been thinking of God as so high above me, that I was distanced from Him. I was feeling as though I was separated from God rather than at one with God.

EXPERIENCE THE PEACE, LOVE AND BLISS I AM

Word for word from God the Father – the unmanifest Source – August 5, 2014

I am the formlessness before there was form that is within every form. I am Life Energy and I am what keeps the ocean current moving, your heart beating, the flowers blooming, the earth rotating, the sun shining and the moon rising. I am pure Life Energy that is pure Peace, pure Love and pure Bliss. I am in each and every one of you.

When you begin to express Me – by feeling more and more of Me (Peace, Love and Bliss) - you become more like My Son, more as Christ Consciousness[1]. I brought Jesus into the world to show you the way back to expressing Me. You lost your way a long time ago. Where there is fear, there is a lack of Me, a lack of self-love. Fear manifests in many different forms[2]. The deeper the fear, the stronger its power and influence over you. This fear may also be what some refer to as the "devil".

Fear is a force that believes in separation. It is also called an ego. It is a perception based on the fear of being separated from Me, your Creator. When you believe in this perception, fear develops. This is truly just an illusion; an illusion created from your mind which cannot possibly perceive otherwise due to the limited nature of its construct. The longer you believe in your fear-based perception, the stronger and more influential it becomes.

The longer you think, feel and behave in ways designed to avoid facing your fears, the more dysfunction and sickness grows. This causes less awareness and less experience of Me (Peace, Love and Bliss). Always, I am equally within you, the same. But, this force, the "devil", this accumulation of fear energy, dominates your perception and unconsciously governs your thoughts, feelings and actions.

This habit of "old" thinking, feeling and behaving as controlled by your perception, creates disharmony, dysfunction and an emptiness which cannot be filled nor ever satisfied. This yearning for something more which is unattainable, continues to grow. A lack of joy for life will eventually develop and deepen.

Begin to adopt a new perception, a new pattern of thinking, feeling and behaving. Stop searching outside of yourself to fill this mysterious and elusive void. Face your fears instead and go within, for you will find the Kingdom of God within you. You will never find your way back to Me until you are willing to face your fears and go within. You may delay this process, which leads to knowing Me, for your free will allows you to do so. But you will do so eventually, so why not now?

Every one of you creates your own life, your own world, by emanating your perceptions of it back to you. You literally create the direct experience of your life. Know that a deeper intellectual understanding of Me, alone, will not achieve a more direct experience of Me.

Expanding Me, which is already within you, is what you need to do and this is all you will ever need to do. Experience the life I chose for you to have. It is far superior to what you could possibly ever achieve on your own. You are here to experience what YOU want to experience AFTER you have first come to Me. You will never reach contentment without Me.

I am communicating through Connie now to give all of you this message directly. I am the Creative Intelligence of Peace, Love and Bliss energy which created all there is. I will give you further recommendations beyond what My Son has given you as of now, for the sole purpose of gaining enlightenment. The full realization of Me is always attained <u>through the experience</u> of Me; through <u>experiencing</u> My Peace, Love and Bliss. Know that I, also, experience the Peace, Love and Bliss that I am, through you. Without you, even I am incomplete.

Find out what your specific fears are. Realize that each and every one of them stems from believing you are a being, separate from Me. You do not know Me, so you misplace your fear onto something or someone else. But, if you knew Me, your fears would vanish. You try to manipulate what you experience, thinking that to do so will solve your problems. But, the only problem you ever have is the forgetting of who I am. So, bypass all of the misguided goals in your life and come straight to Me to achieve lasting happiness. I will bring you more than you could ever begin to know without Me.

I have given Connie the knowledge and understanding through specific experiences throughout her life that have enabled her to be ready to seek Me fully. I have given Mette the knowledge and understanding through specific experiences throughout her life that has enabled her to be ready to seek Me fully. Although they both think they have been ready for many years now, in truth they are only ready as of recently.

Mette has been given a gift directly from Jesus that is a powerful method for developing a more loving heart, fully healed from your many sorrows and pains. All sorrows and pains come from your self-made fears and are a symptom to which you should pay attention. I gave you the symptoms of pain and sorrow as a pathway, so that you may notice the fear that keeps you believing in our separation. Yet, you continue to ignore it and do not realize you are ignoring the path to enlightenment – the realization that we are One and that we are not separate at all.

The Heart Technique for Mette is an effective instrument to help you gain momentum toward experiencing more of your soul's Peace, Love and Bliss. Connie will be teaching how to feel more and more of My Peace, Love and Bliss through helpful action.

There is a daily program in stillness from Mette and a daily program in activity from Connie which are now being given to the world through My Son. If you wish to be happy and grow toward your full potential, seek to develop your soul. Your soul has long been unnoticed within you, waiting to be realized. If you seek it, you will find it. I am your Soul. Seek Me effectively through what Mette and Connie have come to share. This is not a new knowledge, but a road map that will quickly point you toward Me.

[1] The level of awareness and consciousness of Christ. (As defined by God)
[2] Negative emotions, mental and physical imbalances and dysfunctional behaviors. (As defined by God)

Why You Are Not Happy

From God the Father – the unmanifest Source – October 2, 2014
I would like to talk about why people are not happy. People are not happy because they have forgotten who they are. I'd like to tell you who you are.

You are spiritual beings who come directly from Me – pure love energy. I wanted to experience the love I am. I created your physical world and your physical bodies to experience My love through you.

All of you are perfect. You have never, nor could ever, not be perfect. But, you came to believe you were not actors in a play, but the play itself. I want you to expand your understanding (awareness), so you can grow, for your beliefs are keeping you stuck in a rut.

Do you think your spirit dies along with your body? Do you think you are in need of something you do not have? Have you forgotten about why you are here? Instead of being just your human self, living and maintaining your physical life, why not try a different way of life? Are you happy? Are you full? Do you really know who you are? Are you in a state of bliss, peace and joy every moment? If not, why not try something new?

Give your spirit some energy. This includes time, consideration and caring. You spend so much time and energy to have your physical needs and desires met, but they will not make you happy. No matter what you gain in the physical world, it will not make you happy.

The only thing that will make you happy is to get to know your soul. How do you get to know your soul? What is your soul? It is pure love energy. You get to know it by experiencing it, by feeling it. And how do you experience and feel love energy? By giving it – extending it to yourself and to others.

Usually, you live only for your human self. You do not know who you really are. Get to know yourself by sharing your love. I will have Connie give you recommendations for different ways to be an open and active channel of love. Try it for a brief time. If you do not prefer this new way of living, you can always go back to where you are now.

Upcoming Workshops

Upon completion of this book, Jesus asked me to begin yet another book; a workbook to supplement to this one, *"Help From Heaven"*. It will detail the methods given for applying these powerful changes into your everyday life. Choosing rapid spiritual growth is not only desirable, it is highly practical – and available for all who wish to experience it. All it takes is a little help from heaven.

Please check out my website to find out more about these upcoming workshops. Questions and comments are always welcome. I offer phone consultations with beings of your choice, to assist you with medical, personal or spiritual growth issues.

www.HelpFromHeaven.net

I am a licensed Health Practitioner specializing in mercury/environmental detoxification. Too many people struggle with health problems year after year, as I did, not knowing the hidden cause of their ailments. That is why I chose to specialize in mercury toxicity and other environmental poisons. I am near the completion of my book, *"Mercury Madness"*. For more information visit:

www.MercuryMadness.info

THE LIFE PIECE

One afternoon, my friend, Joshua Louis and I were talking to Jesus. Joshua asked Jesus about His life as a carpenter and what items He used to make. This conversation led to this...

**IT HOLDS EVERYTHING YOU NEED
TO KNOW ABOUT LIFE...**

And it was a gift from Jesus Himself...This little piece of wood, about two inches in diameter and shaped like a dome, was once hand made by Jesus Christ. Aside from making tables and chairs, Jesus crafted these little spiritual keepsakes for people. But why? What did this little artifact with such a simple but interesting design mean?

The story is, Jesus was teaching someone one day about the concepts between one's inner and outer qualities. The difference between pure love and fear; the ego and one's true-self - an important lesson to say the least. The man he was teaching, picked up a stick and drew this design in the sand. Jesus, from there, adopted this pattern to help explain His word.

He made many and gave them to people as gifts to remind them of what separates us from the Source in which we're derived from. And of course, most importantly, how to find our way back. Allow the Life Piece to guide you. Regardless of who or what you believe in, know Love is all you need!

The design isn't complex, but extremely rich in meaning. The big dot in the middle represents GOD. There are 14 outer points and 14 inner sections, as well as an outer ring. Throughout history, the number 14 has held significant meaning, as there is a 14 point star marking the place where Christ is believed to have been born.

On the design, the outer points represent your outer qualities; qualities that come from your ego and are fear-based. The lines that run from GOD to the outer points represent how fear and ego pull us away from GOD, which is pure love.

The outer circle represents the ring of fear where all of those outer qualities thrive. The inner sections represent your inner qualities. These qualities come from GOD. They live in your true-self and are the way back to GOD when we find ourselves lost. A mini life roadmap, if you will, to remind you. It's pretty simple, but not always easy. Keep it with you wherever you go. Hold it, look at it and remember what it represents and who made it. May it bring you many blessings!

Joshua Louis

Copyright 2013 The Facility of H.O.P.E. (Helping Other People Evolve)

The Design

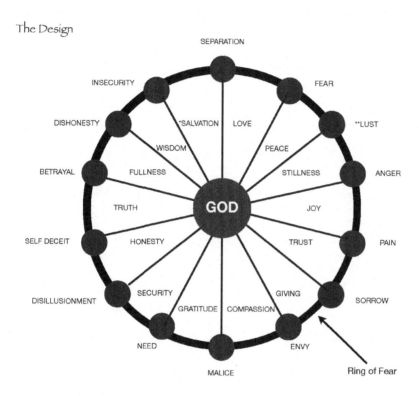

*Salvation- Freedom from fear
**Lust- Any imbalanced desire

Copyright 2013 The Facility Of H.O.P.E.

www.TheLifePiece.com

Made in the USA
Coppell, TX
29 May 2022